A BRIEF HISTORY OF FRANCE

EMPIRES, KINGS, AND REVOLUTIONS

DOMINIC HAYNES

eBook ISBN: 978-1-915710-53-6

Paperback ISBN: 978-1-915710-54-3

Hardcover ISBN: 978-1-915710-55-0

Published by: Dominic Haynes History

CONTENTS

MESSAGE TO THE READER

Before we get started on our journey through the history of France, we wanted to offer you a few tools that we hope will enhance your experience.

Companion PDF: We know that rich historical narratives can be brought to life even more with some visual help. With that in mind, we've created a companion PDF to accompany this book. The PDF contains images of various pieces of art, architecture, and landmarks that we hope will provide you with a more vibrant journey through France's history. Look out for all words in the book with a superscript number, as they will have a corresponding image in the PDF. Scan or click on the QR code below to access the PDF.

A Surprise History Ebook: We value your enthusiasm for history, so we have put together a one-hour-long surprise history ebook. All you need to do to claim it is sign up for our email community, and we'll send it straight to your inbox. You will also be able to join our advanced review team for future books and have a say in what we write about next. Scan or click on the QR code to get access to it.

Thanks for joining us on this journey through France's past. We hope you find it enlightening.

Warmly,

Dominic Haynes History

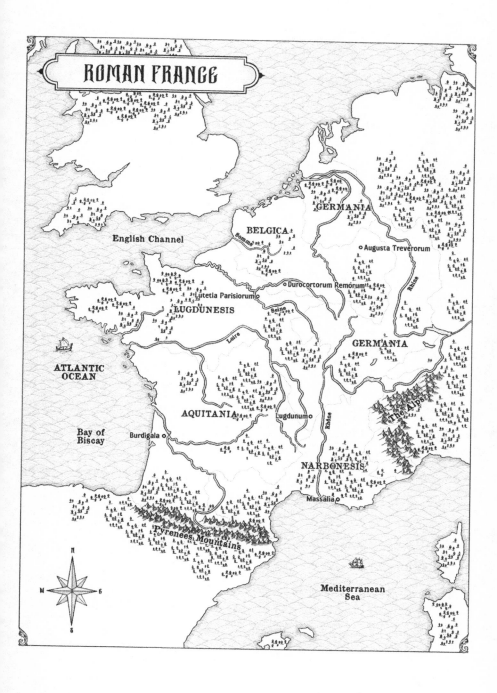

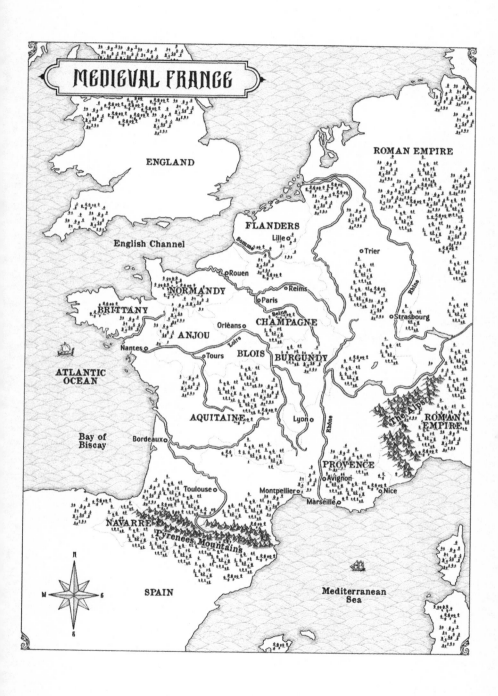

MEDIEVAL FRANCE

ENGLAND

ROMAN EMPIRE

FLANDERS

Lille

Somme

Trier

Rouen

English Channel

NORMANDY

Reims

Paris

BRITTANY

Rhine

Strasbourg

Seine

CHAMPAGNE

Orléans

ANJOU

Loire

Nantes

Tours

BLOIS

BURGUNDY

ATLANTIC
OCEAN

AQUITAINE

Lyon

The Alps

ROMAN
EMPIRE

Rhône

Bay of
Biscay

Bordeaux

PROVENCE

Avignon

Toulouse

Montpellier

Nice

Marseille

NAVARRE

Pyrenees Mountains

Mediterranean
Sea

SPAIN

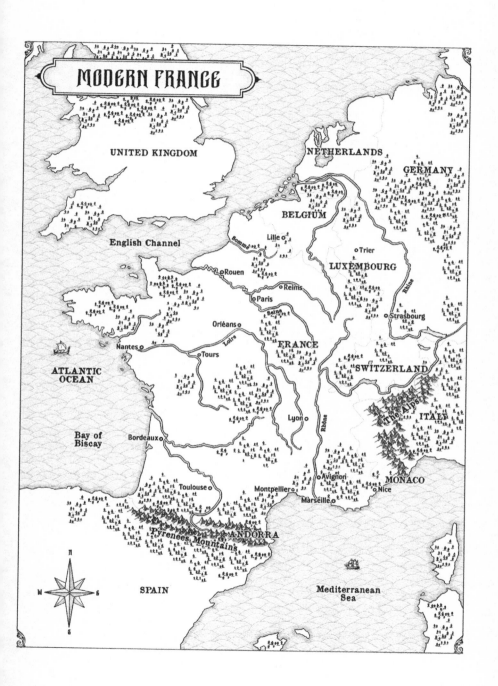

INTRODUCTION

As one of the largest countries on the continent of Europe, France has historically been an integral player in the region, even in its infancy. From its role as the cradle of the Gauls to the host of the splendors of the Louvre, the history of France is a crossroads of all the different cultures that have walked the land.

Today, France sits on the western edge of the European continent. Bound by Germany, Luxembourg, and Belgium to the north, France's other borders are determined mainly by geographic features. To the east and south lie the jagged crags of the Alps and the rolling mountains of the Pyrenees, while the Atlantic Ocean forms the entirety of the nation's western border. Vast, fertile plains sandwiched between all these geographic wonders make up the majority of the French countryside, but the sheer size of the nation allows for a great diversity of soils and climates. Thus, in the same country renowned for cultivating grapes, there are also large crops of wheat, barley, and sugar beets.

As a crucible of culture, politics, and innovation for centuries, France's story reaches beyond a chronological account of events, highlighting the best and worst of what humanity has to offer. This mosaic of triumphs and tribulations, art and upheaval, and enlightenment and resistance forms the nation's unique identity.

We begin in the ancient days of pre-Roman Gaul when the Celtic tribes still roamed the land. We then visit the ghosts of Vercingetorix and his brave resistance against Julius Caesar. From there, explore the Roman footprint that left such indelible marks, shaping the landscape and introducing the seeds of the cities we know today. Yet, it was in the gauntlet of medieval Europe that the French identity truly began to take shape. Clovis and Charlemagne, with their grand visions of a united kingdom, laid the foundation for what would become modern France.

The medieval tapestry unfolds further with the Hundred Years' War, a protracted struggle that tested the mettle of the French spirit. The indomitable Jeanne d'Arc (Joan of Arc) emerged as a beacon of hope, leading the charge that would eventually see the French crown victorious. Later, the Renaissance brought a wave of artistic and intellectual revival, with the splendor of the French court under Francis I rivaling the grandeur of any European kingdom.

As the pages turn, we find ourselves at the crossroads of revolution. The French Revolution of 1789 CE, a seismic upheaval, shook the very foundations of monarchy and heralded the dawn of a new era. Liberty, equality, and fraternity became the rallying cries that echoed across the nation and beyond. The storming of the Bastille and the subsequent rise of Napoléon Bonaparte marked pivotal moments, shaping not only France but the course of European history.

Our narrative, however, is not confined to battles and politics alone; it extends to the salons of intellectuals, the studios of artists, and the streets where revolutions were born. We delve into the Belle Époque, an era of cultural effervescence, and witness the resilience of a nation scarred by the horrors of World War I. The interwar period, a cauldron of artistic innovation and social change, set the stage for the tempest of World War II, where France faced occupation and emerged with the strength to rebuild.

The post-war years ushered in an era of reconstruction and transformation. The birth of the European Union sees France at the forefront of a new vision for collaboration and peace. From existentialist philosophy to the global impact of French cinema, our journey concludes with the vibrant spirit of contemporary France.

This text, though brief, is a light-speed odyssey through time, inviting readers to traverse the landscapes of a nation that has shaped the course of human history. Join us as we unravel the threads that bind the past, present, and future of France, where each chapter tells a story of resilience, revolution, and the enduring spirit of the French people.

1

A CELTIC CANVAS: PAINTING THE LANDSCAPE OF PRE-ROMAN GAUL (3400–58 BCE)

F rance has been marked by human occupation since the Paleolithic Era, as evidenced by the ancient paintings found within the country's vast network of caves. The most famous is the impressive Lascaux cave network near the village of Montignac in the southern-central portion of the nation. Thus, the pattern of humanity's presence in France largely follows that seen in other places around the world. Migratory groups moved in and around the area during the Paleolithic Era and began to settle into more permanent settlements during the Neolithic Era, when agriculture and animal husbandry became more widespread.

There is evidence of several early cultures, beginning at the tail end of the Neolithic Era. The Seine-Oise-Marne (SOM) culture in northern France and southern Belgium dates back to around 3400 to 2800 BCE and is recognized mainly by their stone-lined collective gravesites. Their dead were often interred with arrowheads, ornamental stone pieces, and the occasional copper bead or two.

During the beginning of the Bronze Age, roughly around 2800 BCE, the Bell Beaker phenomenon was also underway. Unlike the SOM Culture, the Bell Beaker groups are identified by a distinctive type of pottery they created: a drinking vessel shaped like an inverted bell. It is generally thought that these cultures might have been migratory groups interacting with one another and settling among local indigenous populations. Since there is no written record, only the archaeological record can speak, which is sadly an oblique form of communication. Whether the Bell Beaker people were their own ethnic and racial group or not remains to be seen, but the kinds of artifacts associated with them have been found not just in France but also as far away as Ireland, northwest Africa, Sardinia, and Sicily.

Another of the earliest cultures present in France was the enigmatic Urnfield culture. Thriving during the Late Bronze Age, not much is known about this group besides its distinctive burial practices: interring their dead in a manner that was a departure from traditional burial customs. Rather than bury their departed kin, the Urnfield culture opted for cremation, a practice involving the burning of the deceased and the placement of their ashes in urns.

These urns were often adorned with intricate designs and spread across central and western Europe, exhibiting a remarkable degree of aesthetic unity. Thriving in regions that now encompass France, Germany, Switzerland, and beyond, these societies engaged in agriculture, metalworking, and trade. Their use of bronze, a testament to humanity's evolving metallurgical skills, became a hallmark of their craftsmanship. Hilltop settlements, strategically fortified, dotted the landscape, reflecting a society cognizant of both communal cooperation and the need for defense in an uncertain time. The interconnectedness of these communities facilitated the exchange of goods and ideas, fostering a vibrant cultural interchange during this era.

Yet, as their moniker suggests, it is with their many necropoli that the Urnfield culture truly speaks across the ages. Their gravesites, vast fields dotted with urns, reveal not only the complexity of their burial rituals but also the societal structures that governed life and death. The presence of personal items, tools, and ornaments alongside the urns hints at a belief in an afterlife replete with familiar comforts. Additionally, the metallurgy used by the Urnfield culture significantly impacted the Iron Age societies that came afterward.

The early Iron Age within French history is frequently divided into the Hallstatt and La Tène periods. As the metals of choice changed from copper and bronze to iron, the Hallstatt culture arose first. Representing a significant archaeological and cultural phenomenon that spanned the Late Bronze Age and Early Iron Age in Europe, this civilization takes its name from the town of Hallstatt in the Austrian Alps. Thriving from roughly 1200 to 500 BCE, it has an observed similarity with later Celtic cultures, and so is frequently deemed to be a proto-Celtic civilization.

Though it began in central Europe, over time, the archaeological and cultural hallmarks of the Hallstatt group spread into France, Germany, the Czech Republic, and Hungary. However, the birthplace of the culture was renowned for two chief resources: salt and iron. Both would prove to be instrumental in the success and survival of its people. The mining of salt, a precious commodity in the ancient world, fielded economic prosperity and extensive trade networks, linking Hallstatt with distant regions and exposing a wide array of people to their way of life. Furthermore, the wealth generated by the salt trade directly contributed to the cultural and technological advancements of the society.

As a result, the Hallstatt culture became notable for its advancements in metalworking, particularly in the production of iron. As mentioned above, iron was supplanting the weaker metals of copper and bronze, so the culture's avid iron production marked a significant technological advantage and provided Hallstatt with superior tools for agriculture, construction, and warfare.

Cultural hallmarks of the Hallstatt include their diverse burial practices. Though evidence of cremation, like that of the Urnfield culture, can be seen in some Hallstatt sites, burial rites often reflected the social status of a given individual. The wealthy elite were interred in elaborate tombs and burial mounds, often referred to as *tumuli*, and accompanied by valuable grave goods like iron objects, pottery, jewelry, and even wagons. The art recovered at such sites is distinctive: intricate metalwork, pottery, and textile designs that show an eye for detail, a dedication to craftsmanship, and an artistic sensibility. The so-called "Hallstatt style" is known for geometric patterns, specifically stylized animals, and other various intricate motifs.

The social stratification evident in death points to a socially complex and hierarchically minded culture. These settlements were likely organized into chiefdoms or rudimentary proto-states with centralized authority controlling the rich resources.

Overall, the Hallstatt culture laid the groundwork for the subsequent La Tène and later Celtic cultures that emerged in France specifically, and Europe generally. Its technological innovations, economic strategies, and social structures shaped the trajectory of European history during the Iron Age.

Despite its contributions and wealth, the Hallstatt culture, like many that came before and after, began to experience a decline in the fifth century BCE. This was primarily due to the depletion of their chief natural resource and export: salt. Their old trading partners were forced to look elsewhere to source the valuable mineral, and the economic prosperity of the culture gradually waned. Eventually, they were supplanted by the La Tène culture. As an aside, rather than one monolithic entity, it is helpful to consider the La Tène as a conglomeration of many small groups that share cultural affinities and characteristics.

Spanning from around 450 to 50 BCE, the La Tène culture is named after the archaeological site of La Tène on Lake Neuchâtel in Switzerland. This cultural phenomenon played a crucial role in shaping the landscape of Iron Age Europe and extended across a vast area encompassing modern-day France, Switzerland, Austria, Germany, the Czech Republic, Hungary, and even parts of the British Isles. The sheer size of the land mass on which evidence of La Tène influence can be found is a testament to the increased interaction and cultural exchange that marked their rise.

One thing that makes the La Tène culture distinct from other entities is the blending of Celtic and Greco-Etruscan artistic sensibilities. Renowned for its distinctive art style, La Tène artifacts[1] are characterized by intricate metalwork, particularly in the creation of weapons, jewelry, and everyday objects. These frequently featured ornate patterns, zoomorphic designs, and swirling motifs, showcasing a high level of craftsmanship and artistic expression.

Much like the Hallstatt and many other ancient cultures, the burial practices of the La Tène varied, but the dead were often sent to their graves with personal items. Warriors were frequently found buried with weapons and armor. However, it isn't warmongering that the La Tène culture is most remembered for; that distinction goes to trade. Like the Hallstatt that they supplanted, the La Tène had extensive trade networks and contacts with neighboring regions, particularly those to the south. There was a fair bit of exchange with Rome, and at first, the relationship between the two seemed cordial enough, with many Roman artifacts recovered at various La Tène sites.

Unfortunately, these friendly relations did not last indefinitely. Rome began to push northward into Europe, encroaching on La Tène territory and constructing various *oppida* in their lands during the first and second centuries BCE. In Roman culture, the oppidum was a more permanent kind of earthwork settlement that was frequently used as a base by legions during times of war. Roman aggression into the heart of Europe continued and increased under the rule of Julius Caesar, but this will be covered later.

Up until this point, the Celts have only been obliquely mentioned. However, they were integral to the development of European history, and the history of France in particular. Furthermore, at times, the Celtic and La Tène cultures have been conflated. To be sure, there are commonalities between the two. Their artistic sensibilities and burial practices come to mind, but it is incorrect to use one as an umbrella term over the other. There was much cultural exchange, warfare, and trade throughout Europe during these centuries, and it can be difficult to parse out one culture from another, especially when the written record is thin.

The Celtic people, though now often associated with the British Isles, did not originate in this region. Furthermore, like the Hallstatt and La Tène cultures, the Celts were never a united state. Instead, they were a collection of chiefdoms and tribes that shared linguistic, religious, and cultural ties. Regrettably, the term "Celt" has at times served as a catch-all term for various inhabitants of Iron Age Europe. However, it may not always be correct, as it oversimplifies complex inter-tribal relations during the time.

Early Celtic culture began developing around 1200 BCE. Though they were influenced by and developed alongside the Urnfield, Hallstatt, and La Tène cultures, their exact origins are hazy. Initially, it was thought that the Celts came from the east and expanded westward through central and western Europe, eventually reaching the British Isles. This was the accepted theory for years and supported by the idea that Celtic languages like Irish, Scots Gaelic, and Welsh are branches of the Indo-European language tree. As an aside, "Indo-European" refers to a vast language family that includes languages spoken by a significant portion of the global population, such as English, Spanish, Hindi, Russian, and more. These languages are believed to share a common ancestry traced back to a hypothetical language called Proto-Indo-European, spoken around 4500–2500 BCE in the Pontic-Caspian steppe region. Historical migrations led to the dispersion of Indo-European languages across Europe and parts of Asia, contributing to the formation of diverse cultures.

This mainstream "Celtic from the East" view largely assigns the Urnfield culture as the progenitor of Celtic civilization and argues that Celts spread outward through the central European cultures of Hallstatt and La Tène into the far-flung regions of Europe: the British Isles to the west and Anatolia to the east. Proponents of the theory often point to the Hallstatt and La Tène cultures as significant cradles of Celtic development. The artifacts recovered, including the artwork and intricate metalwork, as well as the cultural complexities and the broad geographic influence from Central Europe to the British Isles, share affinities with Celtic practices.

However, there are more recent theories like the "Celtic from the West" theory posited by Barry Cunliffe and John T. Koch. This Celtic linguistics and archaeology hypothesis introduces the concept that there is, as the name suggests, a Western origin for Celtic languages and culture. This theory proposes that the Celtic languages, or at least the ancestors of these languages, developed along the Atlantic coast of Europe—specifically in the Iberian Peninsula (modern-day Spain and Portugal), Britain, Ireland, and Armorica (an ancient name for a northwesterly chunk of France that includes the region of Brittany) and subsequently spread to other parts of Europe.

Cunliffe has also suggested that a proto-Celtic language arose during the 3000s BCE and spread through Europe via the Bell Beaker culture. The entire "Celtic from the West" hypothesis has not been wholly embraced by linguists, but it is a fascinating consideration. Supporters often highlight archaeological evidence, especially from the Atlantic Bronze Age (circa 1300–700 BCE), suggesting cultural and trade connections between the Iberian Peninsula and other Celtic regions. Furthermore, some consider shared material culture, such as bronze artifacts and burial practices, indicative of cultural continuity. Lastly, genetic studies analyzing ancient DNA and modern populations have been invoked to support the theory, suggesting genetic continuity between ancient and modern populations in the western part of the Celtic-speaking world.

Though interesting, the "Celtic from the West" theory is not without controversy, and scholars continue to debate the origins and migrations of the Celts. Some argue for a more nuanced view that involves interactions and exchanges between different regions rather than a straightforward origin from one particular area. It is essential to note that our understanding of ancient migrations and cultural developments is continually evolving as new evidence and methodologies emerge. The study of Celtic origins remains a complex and multifaceted field.

The final theory is the "Celtic from the Center" hypothesis. This places the origin of the Celtic languages and associated cultures somewhere between the Atlantic coast and Central Europe—namely, modern France. This idea aligns more closely with traditional views that have often pinned the emergence of Celtic languages to the Hallstatt and La Tène cultures of Central Europe. Noted linguist Patrick Sims-Williams supports this and argues that the "Celtic from the Center" idea explains why the Celtic and Italic languages of the second century BCE are so closely related: the two were in tight geographical proximity. It further answers how Celtic languages were supposedly spoken over a vast distance for an extended period but still managed to avoid major dialectical splits.

While the theory doesn't necessarily dispute later migrations or influences from other regions, it does emphasize the central role of continental Europe, particularly in the early stages of Celtic cultural and linguistic development. It also, while not being a particularly exciting or romantic theory, has the advantage of being a simple explanation. When the Romans pushed into present-day France, or Gaul, as they called it, under Julius Caesar, they encountered a group of people known as *Galli*, or Gauls. These people called themselves *Celtae* (Celts) and were prominent in number. According to the Roman historian Livy, they were the kinsmen of Gauls who had immigrated to the Italian peninsula before Caesar's campaign. The "Celtic from the Center" theory provides a succinct and elegant explanation for what is known from the historical record.

It's important to note that the debate between the "Celtic from the West" and "Celtic from the Center" theories is ongoing within the academic community. Both perspectives seek to unravel the complex origins and migrations of the Celts, and the understanding of Celtic history continues to evolve with new archaeological discoveries, linguistic analyses, and advances in the study of ancient DNA.

As mentioned above, the origins and exact details of the Celtic people are somewhat lost to the mists of time. What is known is that the Celts were a diverse group of Indo-European-speaking peoples who shared cultural traits, linguistic similarities, and, to some extent, a common heritage. They played a significant role in the history of Europe, particularly during the Iron Age. Today, the Celts are associated with migrations that took them to various parts of Europe, including the British Isles, the Iberian Peninsula, and, of course, Gaul (modern-day France).

The bulk of what survives from Celtic culture today is its languages. Celtic is its own branch on the broader Indo-European language family tree. From there, it splits into two: Insular Celtic and Continental Celtic. The latter was largely wiped out by the Roman conquest of Gaul and its surrounding areas and survives only on artifacts. Insular Celtic, on the other hand, lives on in the present day and has split yet again into the Goidelic branch and the Brittonic branch. Goidelic languages include Irish, Scottish Gaelic, and Manx, and are spoken in Ireland, Scotland, and the Isle of Man, respectively. Brittonic (also referred to as Brythonic or Brittanic) languages include Breton, Cornish, and Welsh, which are spoken in Brittany, Cornwall, and Wales. The survival of Celtic languages today is limited, and some, like Manx and Cornish, have nearly gone extinct. Others like Irish, Scottish Gaelic, and Breton are all considered endangered, with Welsh being the only Celtic language not currently in peril. However, there has been a resurgence of Celtic speaking in recent years as those with Celtic heritage seek to reclaim their culture after years of suppression.

Celtic culture in Iron Age Europe was mainly centered around a tribal society with chieftains leading individual tribes. Communities usually fell along kinship lines, with large family groups sticking together. Since this text revolves around France, focusing on the Celts moving forward will broadly highlight those who inhabited Gaul. These people spoke a now-extinct Celtic language known as Gaulish, though some examples survive as inscriptions on archaeological artifacts. These relics, as well as other Celtic art unearthed in Gaul, are characterized by intricate metalwork, particularly in gold and silver jewelry and assorted weaponry. Clearly, the Celts were skilled metalworkers, and their craftsmanship often featured elaborate designs, geometric patterns, and stylized animals.

Celtic religion was polytheistic, with a pantheon of deities associated with natural elements, fertility, and war. Nature and the cycling of the seasons were particularly tied to Celtic religious rituals. Their priestly class, known as Druids, had significant influence in Celtic society and were involved in religious ceremonies and educational and political affairs.

In the popular imagination, Celts are remembered as fierce and fearless warriors, and this has its roots in historical fact. They were known for their martial skills, and their societies often possessed a warrior ethos. Warfare was common in Celtic society—they often waged war amongst themselves and against other cultures. The ideas of honor and bravery in the face of battle and death were highly prized among the Celts. In particular, the Celts in Gaul were known for their prowess in warfare. They used chariots and had skilled warriors who fought with distinctive weapons, including longswords and spears. The Celts were formidable opponents to the Romans, and their conflicts are well-documented in historical accounts. The next chapter will discuss the Gallic Wars and the ensuing Roman conquest.

Aside from the Gauls, though they occupied the bulk of the region, several other communities were present in Iron Age France. There were Germanic tribes that moved in and out of the northeastern portion of France, but the main area of diversity was to the south. The Ligurians were a collection of Neolithic tribes that coalesced in a region on the northwestern coast of the Mediterranean Sea that stretched from Italy into Spain. Though now primarily associated with northern Italy, the Ligurians also inhabited a southern region of Gaul, now referred to as the Provence-Alpes-Côte d'Azur, and the Mediterranean island of Corsica, which in modern times remains under French jurisdiction.

There were also Iberian tribes present near the Pyrenees Mountains along what would later become the border between France and Spain, particularly in a region known as Languedoc-Roussillon. Another influence in the south was the Greek colony of Massalia, now the modern city of Marseille. It was founded in 600 BCE, making it the oldest French city.

Despite the diverse cultures, languages, and individual tribes present throughout France, these would all be absorbed and Romanized in the coming years. Rome was on the march—under the command of Julius Caesar, he and his successors would swallow up the bulk of Europe.

2

THE EAGLE'S EMBRACE: GAUL IN THE GRIP OF ROME (58 BCE– 21 CE)

I n the year 100 BCE, Gaius Julius Caesar was born in Rome to a wealthy noble family. Clawing his way through the political ranks of the Roman Republic, he demonstrated not only administrative skills but also a formidable militaristic mind. His reputation was built during his time as the governor of Hispania Ulterior (present-day Spain) based on many successful campaigns against local tribes. However, by 60 BCE, his homeland's government was in shambles. Recognizing the complexities of Roman politics at the time, he formed an uneasy alliance with Pompey, a celebrated general, and Crassus, a wealthy Roman magnate. This gang of three, or the First Triumvirate, could largely seize control of Roman political life and provide support and protection against their various political adversaries.

In a bid to shore up his political reputation and boost his career, Caesar looked for opportunities in the north. There, the fierce and warmongering Gauls had been a strategic concern for the Roman borderlands for hundreds of years, and military conquest was a means to achieve enduring fame and glory. After all, successful military campaigns were a traditional path for Roman leaders to enhance their prestige and political influence. Furthermore, beyond the aggressive tribes that inhabited the region, Gaul was known for its wealth in the form of fertile lands and valuable resources. A lucrative campaign in Gaul might lead to an acquisition of such riches that would line Caesar's personal pockets and provide him with the means to secure the loyalty of his soldiers and support his political ambitions back home.

Caesar could not very well go out and announce that he was off to plunder Gaul for his personal and professional enrichment, but what he could do was paint it as a defensive maneuver for the good of the Roman nation. Thus, Caesar portrayed his proposed foray into Gaul as a justified invasion to provide Rome with a buffer against potential external threats while eliminating the perceived threats posed by Gaulish tribes. The Roman Senate and citizens largely bought the narrative.

In 58 BCE, Caesar and his four veteran legions departed Rome for Gaul. The initial campaigns from 58 to 56 BCE mostly focused on subduing various Gallic tribes. The Gallic Wars began with the Helvetii, a Celtic tribe from modern-day Switzerland, seeking to migrate westward. Fearing a potential threat to Roman allies in the region, Caesar moved swiftly to block the Helvetii's path. At the Battle of Bibracte in 58 BCE, Caesar decisively defeated the Helvetii and their allies, preventing their migration and establishing Roman dominance in the region.

Following the victory over the Helvetii, Caesar turned his attention to Ariovistus, a Germanic leader of the Suebi tribe who had established himself in eastern Gaul. Caesar was concerned about the growing influence of Germanic tribes in the region. During the same year, he confronted Ariovistus in the Battle of Vosges (Vesontio). The Romans emerged victorious, and Ariovistus fled, solidifying Caesar's control over eastern Gaul.

The Belgae, a coalition of Gallic tribes in northern Gaul, posed a significant challenge to Roman control. Caesar's campaigns in 57 BCE targeted the Belgic confederation, which included tribes such as the Nervii, Atrebates, and Eburones. Despite fierce resistance, Caesar's forces succeeded in subduing the Belgic tribes, expanding Roman influence further into Gaul. At the same time, his lieutenant and the son of his ally, Crassus, Publius Licinius Crassus, worked to bring the regions of Normandy and Brittany under Roman control.

One year later, in 56 BCE, Caesar faced a naval campaign against the Veneti, a seafaring Celtic people inhabiting the coastal region of Brittany. The Veneti had captured Roman envoys and ships, prompting Caesar to respond with force. Caesar's legions, combined with Roman naval superiority, subdued the Veneti in a campaign that highlighted Caesar's adaptability and strategic prowess.

The dust was barely settling from the earlier Gallic War campaigns when Julius Caesar faced a new challenge in 54 BCE with the Revolt of the Eburones, a resilient Celtic tribe nestled in the northeastern reaches of Gaul. The triumphs of previous years, marked by victories over the Helvetii, the

Belgae, and a strategic Germanic threat, had solidified Roman dominance in various parts of the region. However, the actions taken by the Eburones, led by the resourceful chieftain Ambiorix, revealed the complexities and constant work of maintaining control over a vast and diverse territory.

To elaborate, in the aftermath of Caesar's conquests, Roman legions were strategically stationed among the Eburones, ostensibly to preserve order. Tensions often flared when Roman soldiers, in their quest for provisions, incited discontent among the local tribes, but the Romans believed they were on somewhat decent terms with the Eburone people. Ambiorix, on the other hand, saw an opportunity to capitalize on his people's irritation and orchestrated a surprise attack on the Roman camp, catching the unsuspecting soldiers off guard. The chieftain's tactical prowess came to the fore as he skillfully negotiated terms of surrender, only to betray the Romans and initiate an ambush that claimed the lives of Roman commanders Quintus Titurius Sabinus and Lucius Aurunculeius Cotta.

News of the disaster prompted swift action from Caesar, who dispatched reinforcements to quell the revolt and exact retribution upon the Eburones. The Roman response was relentless and unforgiving, leaving widespread destruction in its wake. Ambiorix, recognizing the impending Roman pursuit, chose to go into hiding. He subsequently vanished from the historical record.

Though not altering the overarching trajectory of the Gallic Wars, the Revolt of the Eburones offered a stark reminder of the challenges inherent in pacifying diverse Gallic tribes. It underscored the adaptability of Gallic leaders like Ambiorix, who exploited Roman vulnerabilities and added another layer to the complex dynamics between conquerors and the conquered in ancient Gaul.

Though Ambiorix had been clever, he was, in the end, no match for Julius Caesar. However, the canny Roman tactician soon confronted a far more charismatic and formidable adversary in 52 BCE—Vercingetorix. He was a chieftain of the Arverni tribe, who resided in what is now called Auvergne in central France and were one of the most potent Celtic groups in the area. Vercingetorix used this to his advantage, becoming a leader of the Gallic resistance against Julius Caesar's conquest of Gaul.

Coming to the forefront of Gallic leadership during the latter part of the Gallic Wars, around 52 BCE, Vercingetorix faced the encroaching Roman threat. He emerged as a unifying figure, rallying the notoriously fractious Gallic tribes under a common cause—the defense of Gaul against Roman domination. Focusing the Gallic tribes under his control to mount a concerted effort to cast off the yoke of Roman rule, Vercingetorix's leadership marked a turning point in the Gallic Wars. The tribes, once divided, now coalesced under the banner of resistance.

Demonstrating remarkable military acumen and strategic foresight, he recognized the need for a united front and adopted a scorched-earth strategy that employed a guerrilla warfare approach to deny the Romans access to vital resources. This tactic aimed to exhaust Caesar's legions and disrupt their supply lines while also keeping his troops away from a pitched battle against the veteran Roman legions.

Nevertheless, the two forces ultimately came to blows, and one such instance was the Battle of Gergovia in 52 BCE. Gergovia, the capital city of the Arverni, was perched strategically on a hill and became the focal point of a fierce struggle for supremacy. Guided by Vercingetorix's indomitable will, the Gallic forces initially repelled Caesar's advances, dealing the Romans a significant blow. It is possible that the Celts would not have been able to continually withstand the Roman onslaught, but a twist of fate intervened. Miscommunication on the front lines led to confusion and a partial Roman retreat. Seizing the opportunity, Vercingetorix led a cavalry charge that smashed the Roman lines and dealt Caesar his first actual defeat since entering Gaul.

In the end, his troops lost forty-six centurions and seven hundred legionaries, while the losses endured by the Gauls are unknown. However, one should remember that the main written source of information about the conflict at Gergovia is Julius Caesar's own text, *Commentarii de Bello Gallico* (*Commentary on the Gallic War*). Historians suspect his losses at Gergovia were much heavier, especially since twenty thousand to forty-five thousand Roman troops were engaged in the fighting. Yet, in the end, Caesar won the war and had the opportunity to paint his encounters with the Gauls as favorable to himself and his soldiers. History is, as they say, written by the victors.

In the aftermath of Gergovia, Vercingetorix and his forces withdrew to Alesia, allowing Caesar valuable time to recuperate before he marched once more. A few months after the Gallic victory at Gergovia, the climax of the Gallic Wars began. Fortified and positioned in central France, Alesia was a thriving Gallic city controlled by the Mandubii tribe. Strategically located atop a hill, the city was further fortified by two rivers on either side, as well as deep trenches and stone walls constructed by the Gauls. Recognizing the formidable natural defenses of the town, Vercingetorix chose the city as the bastion for what became his last stand against the advancing Roman legions.

Caesar, on the other hand, cognizant of the challenges posed by a direct assault, believed that a siege was the only sensible answer. He orchestrated the construction of an intricate network of fortifications encircling Alesia—essentially creating a double ring of walls. This masterful engineering feat aimed not only to contain the Gallic defenders within the town but also to thwart any potential reinforcement or escape. Within the walls of Alesia, the Gallic forces braced for a desperate defense against the encircling Roman might.

Vercingetorix knew he was in trouble. With only thirty days' worth of rations squirreled away inside the city, he dispatched pleas for aid to other Gallic tribes. His call was answered, and a massive Gallic relief force assembled to break the Roman encirclement and rescue their compatriots. The ensuing battles were intense, with Roman legions facing the dual challenges of repelling the Gallic relief forces and subduing the defenders within Alesia. Despite the formidable opposition, Caesar prevailed. The Gallic relief forces suffered decisive defeats, and the inhabitants of Alesia, facing starvation and the relentless Roman siege, ultimately capitulated. Vercingetorix, realizing the inevitability of defeat, personally surrendered to Caesar, marking the end of organized Gallic resistance and solidifying Roman dominance over Gaul.

After Vercingetorix was sent away to Rome in chains, only vestiges of the Gallic will to fight remained. However, the Romans spent the next two years stomping out any embers of resistance they caught wind of, and most of the trouble was concentrated in the land between the Seine and Somme rivers in the northwestern portion of Gaul. This land, mainly inhabited by the Bellovaci, another Gaulish tribe, was eventually subdued, as was another uprising at Uxellodunum further south. This fortress, near the present-day town of Vayrac, was subjected to another disastrous siege. The Gauls at Uxellodunum held out until their water supply was depleted, but when they finally surrendered to Caesar, the survivors' hands were cut off as punishment.

Julius Caesar spent the remaining months of the year 50 BCE reorganizing his newly gained territory and setting his affairs in order. Before leaving, he implemented policies to stabilize the region, integrating Gaul into the Roman administrative structure. Roman colonies were established, and veterans of the legions were often settled in Gaul, contributing to the Romanization of the territory.

The revolt of Vercingetorix and the Gallic tribes is still lauded today. His leadership, strategic brilliance, and sacrifice have been romanticized in literature and historical accounts, making him a central figure in the narrative of ancient Gaul and its struggles against the expanding Roman Republic. While the Romans ultimately emerged victorious, the spirited resistance showcased the resilience and surprising unity of the Gallic people in the face of overwhelming odds. The consequences of these events would reverberate through history, shaping the course of Gaul's integration into the burgeoning Roman Empire.

Caesar faced political unrest back home in Rome despite his triumph in Gaul. Rivals viewed him with suspicion and concern and worried about his growing power and popularity. Some senators sought to prosecute him for alleged abuses of power during his consulship and ordered him back to Rome. As Caesar faced the prospect of returning to Rome without the protection of his military command, he was confronted with a difficult choice. He could either disband his army and face potential prosecution or cross the Rubicon River with his legions—an act tantamount to a declaration of war against the Roman Republic.

In January 49 BCE, Caesar made the fateful decision to cross the Rubicon, famously uttering the phrase *"alea iacta est"* ("The die is cast"). By doing so, he violated Roman law and set the stage for a civil conflict. This action plunged Rome into a full-scale civil war between Caesar's forces and those of the Senate and its supporters, led by figures like his former ally, Pompey. The consequences of Caesar's crossing of the Rubicon were profound. The civil war that followed, known as the Roman Civil War or Caesar's Civil War, ultimately led to Caesar's rise to dictatorial power, the end of the Roman Republic, and the beginning of the Roman Empire under his adopted son and heir, Octavian (later known as Augustus).

Once the civil war in Rome was concluded and Caesar emerged victorious, the final chapter of his illustrious Gallic opponent, Vercingetorix, was written. After arriving in Rome following his defeat at Alesia, the charismatic Gaul languished in the Tullianum, a notorious Roman dungeon, for six long years. At one point, during 46 BCE, he was paraded in Caesar's triumphal procession, a traditional

Roman ceremony celebrating military victories. This event showcased the defeated leaders and captured treasures from conquered territories, and Vercingetorix, clad in Roman military attire, was a poignant symbol of the subjugation of Gaul.

After the conclusion of the humiliating procession, the Gallic king was strangled to death at the Temple of Jupiter Optimus Maximus on the Capitoline Hill. This inauspicious fate marked the tragic end of one of the most significant figures in the Gallic Wars, highlighted the harsh realities faced by defeated leaders in the Roman world, and underscored the far-reaching consequences of the Roman conquest of Gaul. Despite his defeat, Vercingetorix is still remembered as a symbol of resistance and as a patron for the quest for freedom against overwhelming odds.

Rome was in a period of unrest and transition during the ensuing years and did not take Gaul in as a formal province until many years later during the reign of Caesar's adopted son and the first emperor of Rome, Augustus (formerly Octavian). However, unrest against the Romans continued for centuries, though none quite ever achieved the traction of Vercingetorix's rebellion. Nevertheless, the integration of Gaul into the Roman Republic (and later the Roman Empire) brought about significant cultural, social, and economic changes. Roman institutions, laws, and customs became prevalent, and Latin became the language of administration. The Romanization process profoundly impacted local cultures, blending Roman and Celtic elements.

Yet despite the political stagnation, the Romanization of Gaul unfolded with transformative vigor, reshaping the very essence of the region. Roman influence manifested prominently in the emergence of sophisticated urban centers adorned with characteristic features such as forums, grand basilicas, temples dedicated to Roman deities, and bustling public baths. Cities like Lugdunum (modern Lyon), Narbo Martius (modern Narbonne), and Arelate (modern Arles) stood as testament to this architectural metamorphosis, becoming hubs of political, economic, and cultural activity.

The Roman road system, epitomized by the remarkable Via Agrippa, wove a network of connectivity throughout Gaul, facilitating the swift movement of people, goods, and ideas. Ingenious aqueducts, with their graceful arches, ensured a reliable water supply to these urban centers, contributing to improved sanitation and urban living conditions. Alongside these feats of engineering, impressive amphitheaters, such as the Amphitheatre of Nîmes[2] and the Arena of Arles[3], showcased Roman architectural innovation, becoming venues for diverse public spectacles and entertainment.

As Romanization advanced, the character of residential areas also transformed. Roman-style villas and townhouses, complete with features like atriums and courtyards, dotted the landscape, reflecting the influence of Roman domestic architecture. Public spaces, including bustling markets and economic centers, became integral to the fabric of Romanized Gaul, fostering commercial exchanges and contributing to the region's economic integration into the larger Roman Empire.

The urbanization and infrastructure development that unfolded in Gaul were not merely physical changes but rather a profound cultural and social evolution. Gaul, once an amalgamation of tribal territories, emerged as a unified and Romanized entity within the expansive tapestry of the Roman Empire.

Individual Gauls became interested in emulating the Roman culture they saw around them, and the adoption of Roman customs and lifestyles became prominent among the Gallic elite. Just as Roman-style villas became in vogue for housing, Latinized dress and social customs also gained popularity, particularly in the growing urban centers. Beyond fashion and architecture, the Gauls, especially those of a higher class, began using the Latin language in lieu of their native Gaulish tongues. While Celtic languages persisted in rural areas, Latin became the language of administration in Gaul, and Latinization was evident in inscriptions, legal documents, and the extensive adoption of Latin by the Gallic upper class.

Alongside the Latin language, Roman legal and political institutions were introduced, shaping the legal framework of Gaul. Roman law and governance structures influenced local administration and provided a unified legal system across the provinces. With Rome eager to integrate the natural wealth of Gaul into their economy, trade networks were expanded, and the introduction of Roman coinage facilitated easier economic transactions.

Among the cultural practices that were adopted, religion played a significant role. Roman religion, chiefly worshipping Roman deities, gained prominence alongside local Gallic religious traditions. The construction of Roman temples and the establishment of cults contributed to the syncretism of religious practices. This bled over into the education of Gallic youth—schools modeled on Roman educational systems emerged, and the spread of Roman literature, philosophy, and art contributed to the ongoing cultural assimilation.

Despite the willingness with which some Gauls adopted Roman characteristics, a subset of the people continued resisting foreign rule, and a long-term Roman military presence was necessary to maintain order and stability in Gaul. Roman legions were stationed in strategic locations, and veteran colonies were established, contributing to the general process of Romanization.

Though Gaul came under Roman control after the Gallic Wars ended in 50 BCE, it was not until the reign of Caesar Augustus that Gaul, in 27 BCE, underwent a significant political reorganization. This was seen as part of the broader administrative changes implemented in the early Roman Empire. Following the end of the Roman Republic and the establishment of the Principate, Augustus sought to streamline governance and secure the empire's stability.

The first such reorganization was the separation of Gaul into three distinct provinces known collectively as the Gallia Comata: Gallia Belgica, Gallia Lugdunensis, and Gallia Aquitania. The southern region of Gaul, which included the old Greek colony of Massalia (Marseille), had been under Roman control for a longer period than the rest of the region and was renamed Gallia Narbonensis during Augustus' reorganization. There is another Roman region in the historical record with the "Gallia" name, Gallia Cisalpina, or Cisalpine Gaul. However, this region, between the Apennines and Alps, is a portion of present-day Italy rather than France. Also, its history differs slightly, and though it was inhabited by Celts, it was incorporated into Rome's territories far earlier than Gaul. Gallia Cisalpina then ceased to be its own region when it was folded into Italy by 42 BCE during Augustus' scrabble for power in the wake of his father's death.

Gallia Belgica was bound to the west and east by the Seine and Rhine rivers, respectively, with its northern border stretching into the Low Countries of present-day Belgium, the Netherlands, and Luxembourg. The province's capital city of Durocortorum became the foundation for the present-day city of Rheims (Reims). Gallia Lugdunensis, known as Celtica by the Greek colonizers to the south, comprised the geographic bulk of Gaul, reaching from its capital city of Lugdunum (modern Lyon) up into the land between the Seine and Loire rivers and stretching to the Atlantic coast. This province included the city of Lutetia Parisiorum, the predecessor of the modern-day metropolis of Paris.

Gallia Aquitania was a smaller province concentrated in the southwesterly portion of Gaul and bound by the Bay of Biscay to the west and the Pyrenees Mountains to the south. Though smaller in overall size than both Belgica and Lugdunensis, Aquitania had strategic significance thanks to both its maritime access and its proximity to the Iberian Peninsula.

Gallia Narbonensis, which encompassed southeastern France, including the famed Côte d'Azur (or French Riviera), saw the first trickles of Roman military presence while assisting the Greek colony of Massalia (Marseille) in 154 BCE against Celtic invaders from the north. Narbonensis was conquered and annexed by the Romans in dribs and drabs from around 125 to 118 BCE, with the final territory stretching from the Mediterranean coast to the Rhône River. Before Augustus renamed Narbonensis, the region was known as Provincia. This legacy is carried on to this day: the southeastern portion of France is commonly referred to as Provence. Notable cities in the region aside from Massalia (Marseille) included the province's capital city of Narbo Martius (Narbonne) and Tolosa (Toulouse).

For the most part, after the conquest, Gaul enjoyed a long period of peace and tranquility that gave the region time to recover and thrive. This was due to the *Pax Romana* (Roman Peace), a prolonged era of tranquility and stability within the Roman Empire during the initial years of the Common Era. Commencing with the ascension of Caesar Augustus to power around 27 BCE, this period of relative peace extended for nearly two centuries until the conclusion of Marcus Aurelius's reign in 180 CE. At its inception, the *Pax Romana* saw Augustus navigating the aftermath of the Roman Republic's upheavals, bringing an end to the recurrent civil strife that characterized preceding decades. Assuming the title of the first Roman Emperor, Augustus inaugurated a new political order, marking the transition from the Republic to the Empire.

Underpinning the *Pax Romana* in Gaul was not just the absence of large-scale military conflicts but also the establishment of pervasive stability facilitated by the Roman legions stationed strategically across the Gallic provinces. Augustus and subsequent emperors engaged in the consolidation and expansion of the empire, fostering territorial stability. The maintenance of internal order was further reinforced by the application of Roman law and governance structures, contributing to a sustained period of domestic peace.

This period is sometimes referred to as "High Roman Gaul." It marks a significant political, social, and cultural shift that shaped the trajectory of Gaul within the Roman world, making it a key region within the empire. Romanization continued throughout this era much as it had in the beginning. Latin continued to be favored over the local languages, and Roman cultural practices were adopted on a wide scale. Most of the urban centers that sprang up, as well as the ones that existed prior to the Roman occupation, began to reflect Roman architectural styles with the use of vaults and arches as well as the adoption of the Greek styles of Doric, Ionic, and Corinthian orders and the Roman inventions of the Composite and Tuscan orders. Examples of Roman structures that have survived into present-day France include the Pont du Gard[4] aqueduct outside the city of Avignon and the Maison Carrée temple[5] in the city of Nîmes. Both sites are located in the southern portion of modern-day France.

Thanks to its natural resources, strategic location, and period of tranquility, Gaul's economy prospered during the *Pax Romana*. Agriculture and trade were staples of economic activity, as was the construction of infrastructure like roads and aqueducts. Gaul already had an established social structure provided by its many Celtic tribes before the Roman invasion and occupation, but the speedy blending of both Gallic and Roman people created a specifically Gall0-Roman elite class, representing individuals of Gallic origin who had largely integrated into Roman society. In a wise maneuver, Augustus and his successors sought to weave local elites into Gaul's Roman-controlled administrative structure, often ensuring that Gallic aristocracy felt appreciated by their Roman overlords. These individuals often held positions of influence with local governance and administration. This strategy aimed to ingratiate the Roman Empire in the eyes of these elites, fostering a sense of cooperation and loyalty among the region's aristocrats toward the Roman state.

Despite the rapid process of Romanization, Gaul retained certain distinct cultural elements, and many Gallic individuals made significant contributions to the military, administrative, literary, and philosophical accomplishments of the larger Roman Empire.

Gallic warriors were highly regarded for their martial skills, and many joined the Roman legions. Gauls played key roles in the Roman military, serving in various capacities and contributing to the expansion and defense of the empire. Some Gauls rose to prominence as military leaders within the Roman legions. Two such individuals were the generals Gnaeus Julius Agricola and Marcus Antonius Primus.

Agricola, born in Gallia Narbonensis around 40 CE, served as the governor of Roman Britain. He was renowned for his military campaigns and chiefly remembered for expanding Roman control in Britain. His expansionary efforts reached as far north as Scotland, leading his troops deep into what Romans referred to as Caledonia. He won various skirmishes and battles against the native tribes of Scotland—namely, the Celtic Caledonians. Agricola constructed forts and roads in England and the lowlands of Scotland, and he was considered incredibly successful by his peers and successors alike.

Primus is slightly less known than Agricola but still played a pivotal role in Roman history. Born in Tolosa (Toulouse) at some point between 20 and 35 CE, he was a Roman general and senator. Shortly after the death of Emperor Nero in 69 CE, he became a critical figure during the Year of the Four Emperors. This succession crisis led to a series of brief but intense civil wars within the Roman Empire, witnessing the rise and fall of four emperors—Galba, Otho, Vitellius, and Vespasian. As various factions vied for control, it ultimately culminated in the establishment of the Flavian dynasty under Vespasian's rule. Primus supported Vespasian and emerged victorious at the Battle of Bedriacum in October of that year, securing Vespasian's rise to the throne.

As mentioned earlier, Gallic individuals were fully integrated into the Roman administrative and political structure. Many Gallic elites held positions of influence within the Roman bureaucracy, contributing to the governance of the empire and fostering a sense of stability and loyalty amongst the Gallic aristocracy. As a result, several notable political figures originated from Gaul, including the emperors Claudius, Caracalla, and Carus. Claudius and Caracalla both hailed from Lugdunum, while Carus was born in Narbonensis.

Gauls also made notable contributions to literature and philosophy within the Roman context. Gallic writers and philosophers, often bilingual in Latin and their native Celtic languages, participated in the broader intellectual milieu of the Roman Empire. The novelist Gaius Petronius Arbiter, known colloquially as Petronius, hailed from Massalia (Marseille) and was active during the reign of Nero. He was ultimately accused of treason, and according to the Roman historian Tacitus, he was arrested and committed suicide before he could be executed. Sextus Julius Frontinus, the author of the technical text on Rome's aqueducts, *De aquae-ductu*, is also thought to be from Gaul–Narbonensis.

Two other well-known writers from Gaul were Decimus Magnus Ausonius (known simply as Ausonius) and Rutilius Claudius Namatianus. Both these men were active during the later period of the Roman Empire. Ausonius, a poet, rhetorician, and teacher, hailed from Burdigala (Bordeaux) in the Gallic province of Aquitania. His most influential position was that of tutor to the future Emperor Gratian. However, he is best remembered for his keen observational and descriptive skills that enabled him to pen the illustrative poem "Mosella" about the Moselle River in present-day northeastern France and Luxembourg.

Rutilius Claudius Namatianus was a poet and politician from the southern portion of Gaul, likely Tolosa (Toulouse) or Pictavium (Poitiers). He lived and worked during the fifth century. Best known for his poetic work titled "De Reditu Suo" (On His Return), a lengthy poem that describes his journey from Rome to his native Gaul and reflects on the decline of the Roman Empire, Namatianus also held the office of prefect in Rome and later served as a consul. His career faced challenges due to political turmoil and the changing fortunes of the Western Roman Empire, but his poetic works provide valuable insights into the social, political, and cultural aspects of the declining Roman world during the early fifth century.

However, despite the cultural integration, relations between the Gauls and the Romans were not always positive. One such example is the Florus-Sacrovir Revolt—a resistance against Roman rule during the early years of Emperor

Tiberius' reign in 21 CE. Led by Gallic leaders Julius Florus and Julius Sacrovir, members of the Treveri and Aedui tribes, respectively, the main goal was to seek greater autonomy for their region, and theirs was not the last of the Gallic rebellions. As the Roman Empire entered its final centuries in a death spiral, Gaul repeatedly attempted to assert greater independence and autonomy, both within and without the empire's framework.

3

NAVIGATING THE SHADOW OF ROME'S FALL (21–496 CE)

B oth Florus and Sacrovir were Roman soldiers and used their connections within their army to sow discontent among their compatriots as well as within the Gallic tribes. The rebellion gained momentum with initial successes, capturing Roman settlements and garnering support from local tribes. However, Rome's response, led by the decisive actions of General Gaius Silius, swiftly turned the tide. Facing military defeat and internal discord, Florus and Sacrovir chose to end their lives.

The Roman retaliation was severe, quashing the uprising and reinforcing Roman authority in Gaul. In response to the Celtic Druids' support of the rebellion, Tiberius banned Druidic practices throughout the Roman Empire, forcing the Celtic religious way of life underground. The revolt's suppression served as a cautionary tale, underscoring the struggles of resisting the might of the Roman Empire and the consequences for those who dared to challenge its rule.

However, even Tiberius' actions did not entirely crush Gallic resistance. Furthermore, as the years progressed, Rome's power was waning. The height of the Roman Empire had passed, and it was becoming increasingly apparent to tribes both inside and outside Rome's borders. In the third century, a Roman general named Marcus Cassianius Latinius Postumus rose to prominence and played a crucial role in establishing a breakaway state known as the Gallic Empire. This huge affront to Roman authority coincided with the Roman Crisis of the Third Century.

The Crisis of the Third Century, also known as the Imperial Crisis, was a tumultuous period from 235 to 284. At its core was a relentless cycle of political upheaval marked by a rapid succession of emperors. This era saw the ascension and fall of rulers through military support, leading to an unsettling lack of stability and a weakened central authority. Amid this political turmoil, formidable military challenges arose on multiple fronts. Germanic tribes worried Rome's northern borders, the Sassanian Empire loomed in the east, and internal conflicts among Roman legions posed significant threats. The military, in turn, gained unprecedented influence, with the loyalty of legions shifting with the changing tides of leadership.

Economically, the empire grappled with a series of crises. Rampant inflation, devaluation of currency, and burdensome taxation created financial hardships for the state and its populace. Trade and agricultural productivity declined, exacerbating the economic woes that permeated Roman society. Territorially speaking, the crisis witnessed the gradual fracturing of the Roman Empire. The emergence of short-lived independent entities like the Gallic Empire challenged the traditional unity of the state. Simultaneously, the Cyprian Plague, raging from 249 to 262, further strained the empire by significantly reducing its population.

Returning to the establishment of the Gallic Empire, Postumus worked in the Roman province of Germania. This area, which encompassed chunks of present-day Germany, Poland, the Czech Republic, Slovakia, Hungary, and Austria, was located east of Gaul. History has characterized Postumus as an opportunist, and with the *Pax Romana* a relic of the past, he was ready and eager to capitalize on the general political unrest rippling through the Roman Empire.

His moment to strike presented itself in 260. Emperor Valerian was captured by the Persian King Shapur, leaving his son and co-emperor, Gallienus, in charge. Many deeply questioned the young man's ability to govern the vast Roman Empire, and Postumus used this moment of uncertainty to make his move. Taking his loyal legion to Colonia Agrippina (modern-day Cologne), he surrounded the garrison, serving as the home of both the praetorian prefect Silvanus and the youngest son and heir of Gallienus, Saloninus.

Gallienus, occupied with threats from the east, was hardly in a position to answer the aggression from Postumus in the west. With no aid on the way, Silvanus and Saloninus saw no way forward and surrendered to Postumus. Both were summarily executed, after which Postumus declared himself the emperor of the Gallic Empire. This new breakaway state encompassed most of Gaul and pieces of Germania, and even spread into Britain. He found willing support from the populations of these areas as well as from the Roman legions stationed in Germania.

Despite being primarily made up of Gallic populations, Postumus' new kingdom was distinctly Roman in flavor. He took up residence in Augusta Treverorum (present-day Trier), establishing it as his capital city. After implementing a senate, two consuls, and various other features of Roman governance and culture, he set about fortifying Gaul. He was most interested in protecting his empire from roving Germanic tribes, specifically the Franks and the Alemanni, rather than expanding his territory. He never tried to execute an invasion into Rome and was seemingly only interested in improving life for the Gallic peoples.

By the mid to late 260s, Gallienus was able to turn his attention back to the West and began a concerted effort to reclaim Rome's lost lands. However, the Roman emperor was injured, and his chief commander defected to Postumus's cause, greatly damaging the Roman position. Ultimately, in 268, both Postumus and Gallienus were assassinated by their respective troops due to either discontent or conspiracy. The Gallic Empire managed to limp along for a few more years after Postumus' demise, ruled by a brief succession of short-lived leaders. The Gallic Empire's territory was gradually chipped away, with both Spain and Britain returning to Rome's open arms. Gaul finally fell into the hands of Emperor Aurelian in 274, deposing the last Gallic emperor, Tetricus.

By now, Rome was economically and governmentally wobbling. Emperor Diocletian came to power a decade after the end of the Gallic Empire and attempted to staunch the bleeding. Hoping to end the Crisis of the Third Century, sweeping administrative reforms were enacted to fortify the foundations of the Roman Empire. These transformative measures, known as the Tetrarchic Reforms, were a meticulous restructuring of the administrative and political life in the Roman Empire. He managed to stave off the ultimate collapse of his ancestors' empire for another two centuries.

At the heart of these reforms was the establishment of the Tetrarchy, a visionary system that divided the Roman Empire into distinct Eastern and Western realms. Each half was further subdivided under the auspices of an Augustus, or senior emperor, and a Caesar, a junior emperor. This strategic division aimed to enhance governance by creating a coordinated rule, ensuring a smoother transition of power through designated successors. Diocletian became the Augustus of the eastern half with Galerius as his Caesar, while Maximian took up the mantle of Augustus in the west alongside his Caesar, Constantius Chlorus. The empire was now essentially chopped into four districts, and the main administrative center was moved over one thousand miles east to the city of Byzantium. This city would, in 330, be renamed Constantinople in honor of Emperor Constantine and re-christened as İstanbul in 1930.

Administratively, the empire underwent a significant transformation. Diocletian introduced the concept of dioceses, conglomerates of provinces overseen by appointed officials known as *vicarii* (*vicarius,* if singular). This innovative administrative tier facilitated centralized control and streamlined communication between the provinces and the imperial center. Within these dioceses, provinces retained their identity but underwent adjustments to their numbers and borders, offering a nuanced administrative landscape.

Diocletian instituted praetorian prefectures to further decentralize power and enhance governance, appointing one for each Tetrarch, each presiding over a group of dioceses. The praetorian prefects, occupying pivotal roles, were entrusted with both military and civilian administration within their designated regions. This marked a deliberate move towards separating civil and military authority, ensuring a more defined structure. Furthermore, each *vicarius* answered to one of the four praetorian prefects, illustrating Diocletian's resolve to create a clear hierarchy of authority within Rome.

Diocletian's administrative reforms were only a part of the broader Tetrarchic Reforms, and they ushered in a period of temporary stability. Through the separation of powers, refined governance structures, and a meticulous approach to administrative efficiency, the Roman Empire sought to confront the multifaceted issues that had imperiled its unity and strength. The tides of history would reveal that while these measures offered respite, the underlying challenges endured, ultimately contributing to the gradual decline of the Western Roman Empire.

Nevertheless, his innovative political structure did not have the staying power to continue long after he stepped away from his throne. The decline of the Tetrarchy began as soon as Diocletian retired from his position as Augustus in 305. Tensions among the Tetrarchs became apparent soon after he stepped back, and petty disputes over authority and influence escalated. The structure of the Tetrarchy relied on the smooth transition of power between the Augusti and designated Caesars, but internal rivalries threatened its stability.

Though the larger political and administrative structure of the empire was in flux, the Gallic provinces enjoyed a period of relative influence and stability following the Diocletian reforms. Essentially, Rome, in an attempt to keep its borders secure, decided to keep the Rhine River region heavily fortified against the Germanic tribes. The renewed importance of this waterway, which served as an aqueous border between Gaul and Germania, meant that Gaul and its citizens enjoyed more significant influence and representation within the empire. A praetorian prefect was stationed in the area, and many emperors made it a point to dwell among the Gallic peoples for a portion of their reigns, including, most notably, Emperor Constantine I.

The Tetrarchy and its succeeding emperors had managed to stretch Rome's lifespan out, but toward the end of the 300s, severe economic challenges and external threats arose. Simultaneously, the Western Roman Empire grappled with internal strife, political fragmentation, and relentless invasions by Germanic tribes and the formidable Huns from Central Asia. By 395, the sons of Theodosius I—Arcadius and Honorius—ascended to power over the Eastern and Western Roman Empires, respectively. Their rule formalized the division, marking the point of no return. The death of Theodosius I, who had temporarily reunified the empire, ushered in a new era where each emperor would now steer his own course.

Gaul became a focal point of political and military developments. The Tetrarchic Reforms and the subsequent civil wars among claimants to the imperial throne had repercussions in Gaul, with power struggles, shifting allegiances, and intermittent periods of instability. As the fourth and fifth centuries progressed, the Germanic tribes grew more and more bold. Groups such as the Vandals, Alans, and Visigoths crossed the Rhine and infiltrated Gallic territories. Cities were sacked, and borders were left undefended, gradually eroding the concept of Roman authority in the region.

In 410, the Visigoths, under King Alaric, famously sacked Rome, marking a symbolic turning point in the diminishing power of the Western Roman Empire. Gaul, situated on the empire's fringes, bore the brunt of these invasions. The city of Augusta Treverorum (Trier), for example, an important Roman administrative center, faced significant upheaval. The decline of the Roman administrative structure and the weakening of central authority led to a degree of regional autonomy in Gaul. Sensing the changing tides, local elites began asserting more control over their territories. This period witnessed the emergence of regional leaders who often operated independently of the distant imperial center.

By 418, Frankish and Burgundian tribes were well-established west of the Rhine, and the Visigoths were comfortably ensconced in Aquitania (Aquitaine) to the south. Luckily for the Gall0-Romans, these Germanic tribes had decent relationships with the Romans, and their aggression was generally checked by a prominent general in the region: Flavius Aetius. However, with his passing in 454 and the loss of Roman holdings in Northern Africa to the Vandals, Roman control in Gaul all but evaporated.

The Visigoths stepped into the void, and through the latter half of the fifth century, Visigothic kings steadily expanded their territories, swallowing up a large swath of southern Gaul. The last Roman-held outpost in Provence ultimately fell to the Visigoths in 476. The Burgundians, not to be outdone, grew their territories westward, while the Franks occupied much of the northern portion of Gaul. Naturally, this kind of unrest and turbulence was difficult for Gaul and its inhabitants. Skirmishes forced families to uproot and flee south into Roman-controlled areas as refugees where circumstances were little better than those of the dispute-laden land they had just left. Infrastructure was severely damaged by conflict, while social and administrative hierarchies dissolved.

By the late fifth century, Gaul underwent a profound transformation with the arrival of the Franks, a Germanic tribe led by Clovis. Clovis united the Frankish tribes and established a powerful kingdom in northern Gaul. His conversion to Christianity in 496 marked the beginning of a Frankish monarchy that would play a significant role in shaping the medieval history of the region.

With the arrival of the Franks, the time of the Romans was brought to an end. In essence, during the decline of the Roman Empire, Gaul experienced a complex interplay of internal power shifts, external invasions, and the emergence of new political entities. The legacy of this period laid the groundwork for the medieval kingdoms that would emerge in the former Gallic territories, contributing to the diverse and dynamic history of the region. A new influence came to the region and combined with the Gallic and Roman elements that were present to steadily create its own unique culture. Though the fall of Rome left a gaping vacuum in Europe, Gaul under the Franks was poised to launch the region into the medieval era by way of the Dark Ages.

4

OF MEROVINGIANS AND CAROLINGIANS (496–771 CE)

The shadow of Rome's eagle wings receded over the Alps, and Gaul, the long-held daughter of the empire since the days of Julius Caesar, was left to fend for itself. The land was now largely a patchwork of various Germanic tribes, and though the Visigoths initially held primacy, other groups like the Burgundians and Alemanni were present. However, beginning in the latter half of the fifth century, the Franks came to dominate the region.

Originating as a confederation of Germanic tribes, the Franks moved into Gaul during the tumultuous Migration Period (also known as the time of the Barbarian Invasions). This period is seen by historians as a transitional phase between the era of Late Antiquity and the Early Middle Ages. The Franks at this time were lumped into three main branches: the Ripuarians, the Salians, and the Chatti (Hessians). These groups were all linguistically and culturally connected but politically independent of one another.

The Ripuarian Franks mostly established themselves in the region of the Rhine River, though they also inhabited the areas around the Moselle and Meuse rivers to the west. Another group of the tribe, the Salian Franks, chiefly occupied the Atlantic coast and around the Somme River. The Chatti mostly stayed in present-day Germany in the region now known as Hesse. For the most part, the Franks operated as individual kingdoms, forming small independent clusters in the regions they dominated.

Even though Roman influence was virtually gone, the Germanic tribes, the Franks included, were still quite Romanized in their behavior. After all, Rome had been the dominant power in the region for centuries. Its influence would not be so easily erased or replaced. As a result, many of the Germanic tribes had become Christian thanks to the Romans, albeit most of them, including the Burgundians and Visigoths, adhered to a branch of Christianity known as Arianism. This sect was viewed as heretical by most Romans, who believed it was better to still be a pagan than to espouse heresy. The Franks, however, remained pagan, which would prove significant in time.

By the late 400s, the Salian Franks were governed mainly by one man, King Childeric I, who passed the throne to his son when he died in 481. Clovis, also called Chlodovech or Chlodwig in his native tongue of Frankish, proved to be a capable leader, and could draw many to his banner. As he began slowly uniting all the disparate Frankish kingdoms, he consolidated authority over territories that would later comprise parts of present-day France, Belgium, and Germany.

In 486, Clovis's military prowess was evident in his triumph at the Battle of Soissons, a decisive victory that secured his dominance over northern Gaul by vanquishing the last Roman ruler in the region, Syagrius. Having ruled a small Roman rump state known as the Kingdom of Soissons sandwiched between Frankish and Alan holdings in northern Gaul, Syagrius was the last vestige of the once-omnipresent Romans. Clovis secured most of Gaul, pressing the Visigoths south into Spain. However, his legacy extends beyond military conquests to a pivotal moment of religious significance.

Around 496, during a pivotal battle against the Alemanni, Clovis solemnly vowed to convert to Christianity if fortune favored him. Victorious, he fulfilled his vow, though his conversion was notably to Nicene Christianity rather than to Arian Christianity, and this held profound political implications, which will be discussed anon.

As a brief aside, we will quickly elucidate the differences between Nicene and Arian Christianity. In the early centuries of Christianity, a theological rift emerged, marking a defining moment in the Church's history. The dispute between Nicene Christianity and Arian Christianity centered on the nature of the Holy Trinity and the relationship between God the Father and Jesus Christ. Nicene Christianity, rooted in the Nicene Creed formulated at the First Council of Nicaea in 325, affirmed the complete divinity of Jesus Christ, declaring him to be "of one substance with the Father." This doctrine, championed by figures like Athanasius, emphasized the consubstantiality of God the Father and God the Son, asserting their shared divine essence and eternal co-existence.

On the other hand, Arian Christianity, named after the priest Arius, rejected the Nicene Creed. Arius proposed that Jesus Christ, while divine, was a created being, distinct from God the Father. Using the term *homoiousios* to signify similarity but not the identity of substance, Arianism introduced a form of subordinationism, suggesting that the Son was subordinate to the Father both in essence and time. This theological discord sparked debates and controversies within the Roman Empire, with emperors at times favoring one side over the other.

Ultimately, Nicene Christianity prevailed as the orthodox position, solidifying its ascendancy through subsequent councils, including the First Council of Constantinople in 381. The Nicene Creed, emphasizing the consubstantiality of the Father and the Son, became foundational for mainstream Christian denominations.

Arian Christianity was at a crossroads, grappling with the consequences of the council's decisions that firmly endorsed Nicene orthodoxy. The council not only reaffirmed the Nicene Creed but also expanded upon it, addressing controversies related to the divinity of the Holy Spirit. This marked a significant setback for Arianism, as the theological landscape tilted decisively towards Nicene formulations.

Despite the council's stance, Arianism did not vanish overnight. Resilient pockets of Arian communities persisted in certain regions, and the fate of Arian Christianity remained closely entwined with the shifting currents of political influence. In some instances, rulers continued to lend support to Arianism, contributing to variations in its fortunes across different regions of the Roman Empire.

Successive ecumenical councils, such as the Council of Ephesus in 431 and the Council of Chalcedon in 451, further clarified and solidified Nicene orthodoxy. These councils addressed Christological controversies, leaving little room for Arian interpretations. The decline of Arian influence was also evident in the diminishing support from political and ecclesiastical authorities.

While Arianism persisted among certain Germanic and barbarian tribes, especially the Visigoths, it faced challenges as these regions underwent their own transitions. Over time, some Arians adapted their beliefs, moving towards Unitarianism, a departure from classical Arianism.

In the broader Christian landscape, Arian Christianity gradually lost its prominence. While remnants of Arianism persisted for a time, its status as a major theological contender diminished. The influence of Nicene orthodoxy became the norm in most Christian communities, marking a transformative shift in the theological currents that shaped the evolving Christian thought in the post-Constantinople era.

Returning to Clovis' personal conversion to Christianity, this was a crucial and transformative event in the history of the Franks and, more broadly, the early medieval history of France and Europe. Clovis, the first king of the united Frankish tribes and founder of the Merovingian dynasty, played a pivotal role in shaping the destiny of the Frankish Kingdom.

As noted earlier, the conversion likely took place around the year 496. The primary account of Clovis' conversion is provided by the Gall0-Roman medieval chronicler Gregory of Tours in his work *Ten Books of Histories,* sometimes referred to as the *History of the Franks.* The reader should be cautioned to remember that the veracity of Gregory's account and his purpose in writing remain unclear to present scholars. Nevertheless, according to Gregory, Clovis, facing a critical moment in the battle against the Alemanni, vowed to convert to the Christian faith if victory was granted to him. Miraculously, the tide of battle turned in Clovis' favor.

True to his vow, Clovis embraced Christianity. In a ceremony held at Rheims (Reims) in northeastern Gaul, he was baptized by Saint Remigius, the Bishop of Rheims. The conversion of Clovis was not only a personal religious transformation but had profound implications for the Frankish Kingdom.

Clovis' decision to convert to Christianity was not solely a spiritual choice; it held considerable political significance. At the time, Gaul had a significant Christian population, and Clovis' adoption of Christianity aligned him with the religious beliefs of a considerable portion of his newly minted subjects. This conversion strengthened his legitimacy as a ruler and facilitated better integration with the Romanized population of Gaul. Furthermore, Clovis' embrace of Nicene Christianity, as opposed to Arian Christianity, marked an alignment with the orthodoxy professed by the Roman Church. This alignment enhanced his diplomatic ties and alliances with other Christian rulers and the powerful papacy. As an aside, moving forward, the text will begin referring to Gaul as Francia, or the land of the Franks.

Clovis' conversion set a precedent for the Frankish monarchy, establishing a tradition of Christian rulership that would endure for centuries. The Merovingian kings who succeeded Clovis would continue to be patrons of the Church, contributing to the Christianization of the Frankish Kingdom and laying the foundation for the subsequent Carolingian dynasty's deep relationship with the Church. His strategic expansion of the kingdom through military conquests and alliances roughly formed the rudimentary geographic borders for present-day France.

As has been implicitly mentioned already, Clovis was the founder of both France and the Merovingian Dynasty, a pivotal ruling family from the fifth to the eighth centuries. Though history knows Clovis as its originator, the dynasty takes its name from Merovech, the semi-legendary patriarch associated with the early days of the family. The historical narrative surrounding Merovech is enshrouded in a blend of facts and mythological elements. According to the lore, Merovech's birth was marked by an extraordinary union between a Frankish queen and a sea creature, often portrayed as a sea monster. In reality, the Merovingian Dynasty was officially established by Clovis I, who ascended to become the first king of all the Franks in 509.

As discussed previously, Clovis' reign, spanning from 481 to 511, brought about the unification of disparate Frankish tribes under a single ruler. Following Clovis's death, the Merovingian Kingdom adhered to the Frankish tradition of partible inheritance rather than primogeniture, leading to the division of the realm among his four sons: Theuderic, Clodomir (Chlodomer), Childebert, and Chlothar (Chlotachar). This division gave rise to distinct sub-kingdoms, each ruled by a Merovingian king. However, internal strife and power struggles among these sub-kingdoms weakened the centralized authority of the dynasty. Furthermore, the territorial chunks handed to his sons did not account for any preexisting legal, ethnic, geographical, or cultural partitions. Instead, the only stipulation was that the portions be of "equal value." Borders between the brothers were messy, leading to more problems. Nearly all the brothers' kingdoms were separated parcels of land—Clodomir's kingdom in the Loire Valley was the only one that did not consist of unconnected bits of territory.

Theuderic I, Clovis's eldest, ascended to power over the eastern territories, including Metz and Rheims. His reign, from 511 to 533, witnessed military triumphs against the Thuringians and the Burgundians, though internal familial challenges colored his rule. Theuderic I met his end in 533. Clodomir, the second son, inherited the majority of the Loire Valley region, which included Orléans, Tours, and Nantes. His rule, spanning from 511 to 524, saw military engagements against the Visigoths and Burgundians. A tragic turn of events occurred in 524 during the Battle of Vézeronce, where Clodomir lost his life.

Childebert I received the kingdom of Paris, encompassing parts of the Seine and Loire Valleys. His reign, extending from 511 to 558, involved continued conflicts with the Burgundians and Visigoths. Childebert I played a role in the overthrow of the Visigothic king, Amalaric, and passed away in 558. Chlothar I, the youngest son, initially ruled Soissons in the northwest and a piece of Aquitaine.

Whenever one of the brothers died, their kingdom was further split among the surviving brothers. In the end, only Chlothar I remained, inheriting his brothers' holdings and reuniting his father's lands once again under one crown. Chlothar I continued the expansion of the kingdom and passed away in 561.

However, it seems Chlothar's sons did not learn any lessons from their father and uncles. Upon Chlothar's death, the kingdom was once again parceled out into fourths. There was an undue amount of strife, infighting, and fragmentation in the generations that followed. Sibling rivalries and conflicts over inheritances were common among the Merovingian heirs, and the competing interests of different branches of the royal family often led to open conflicts and power struggles that harmed the ability of the Merovingian kingdoms to truly thrive.

As the Merovingian kings faced internal squabbling, real political power shifted to the Mayors of the Palace. Originally, these figures were the household managers for the royal family, but over time, they became more of a "power behind the throne" rather than a simple administrative body. The decline of Merovingian authority continued, and by the mid-eighth century, the dynasty had become largely symbolic, with the Mayors of the Palace holding effective control.

One such example was Charles Martel, renowned as "Charles the Hammer," who emerged as a pivotal figure in European history during the eighth century. Born around 688 CE into the influential Carolingian family, he was the illegitimate son of Pepin (Pippin) of Herstal, the Mayor of the

Palace for the eastern Frankish kingdom of Austrasia. Upon his father's death in 714, Charles, as a bastard, was neglected as a potential heir. In fact, according to Pepin's wishes, his widow Plectrude was to govern his lands until his three legitimate grandchildren came of age since his legitimate sons were all dead.

Plectrude had Charles imprisoned, but he managed to escape, rally troops to his cause, and achieve remarkable military successes against the rival western Frankish kingdom of Neustria. Plectrude and the Austrasians submitted to Charles, and in 719, he defeated the Neustrians at Soissons, becoming the de facto ruler of the Franks and bringing the northern half of Francia firmly under his control. He went on to invade the southern half of Francia, making incursions into Aquitaine. Aside from fighting fellow Franks, Charles also spent a large amount of time battling other Germanic tribes like the Frisians, Saxons, and Bavarians.

One of Charles Martel's most celebrated military feats occurred in 732 at the Battle of Tours (also referred to as the Battle of Poitiers), where he successfully halted the advance of Islamic forces of the Umayyad Caliphate led by Abdul Rahmān Al-Ghafiqi (Abd al-Rahmān al-Ghafiqi). Essentially, Umayyad expansion had been swelling in Europe since their conquests across the Iberian Peninsula in the early 700s, and Charles put a stop to their expansion.

As the Umayyad forces pressed northward into Francia, Charles Martel, as the Mayor of the Palace and de facto ruler of the Frankish Kingdom, assumed leadership over the defensive efforts and strategically positioned his forces to counter the formidable cavalry charges of the Umayyad army. In October, the forces collided somewhere between the cities of Tours and Poitiers in Aquitaine, exacting heavy casualties on both sides. Charles Martel's disciplined infantry, comprised of heavily armed and well-organized warriors, withstood the onslaught of the Umayyad cavalry. Ultimately, the Frankish forces emerged victorious, and Abdul Rahmān Al-Ghafiqi perished in the conflict.

The Battle of Tours is often hailed as a turning point in European history. Charles Martel's triumph halted the Umayyad Caliphate's advance into Western Europe and prevented the spread of Islam in the region. Though the battle did not expel the Umayyads from the Iberian Peninsula, it kept them south of the Pyrenees. It played a crucial role in shaping the political and cultural trajectory of medieval Europe. This pivotal moment is sometimes referred to as the "Battle that Saved Europe," it contributed to the consolidation of Frankish power and set the stage for the next phase of Frankish rule.

Furthermore, in his capacity as Mayor of the Palace, a role traditionally linked to overseeing the royal household, Charles Martel deftly navigated the intricate political land-scape. Over time, Mayors of the Palace, including Charles and his father, amassed considerable power, overshadowing the now nominal Merovingian kings and contributing to the stability of the Frankish Kingdom amid internal discord and external threats.

Charles Martel's legacy extends beyond his military exploits, though his successful campaigns against neighboring Germanic tribes and rebellious Frankish nobles further consolidated his authority and unified more and more of Francia. When he died in 741, his sons, Pepin (Pippin) the Short and Carloman, were left to continue his legacy.

Inheriting a realm that Charles Martel had effectively governed as Mayor of the Palace, the brothers sought to legitimize their rule and secure support. However, in 747, Carloman renounced his titles and joined a monastery in Rome, leaving his brother in charge of Francia. Ambitious like his father, Pepin was not content to remain merely the mayor and do the work of a king while another claimed the title. He sought the crown for himself and began to form a close alliance with the Catholic Church. In 750, he sent a letter to Pope Zacharius pleading his case. He believed that the Church would not want a king with no power, and Pope Zacharius readily agreed and commanded that the current Merovingian king, Childeric III, be deposed. The following year, 751, Pepin was anointed as the king by Archbishop Boniface at Soissons, while Childeric III was sent to live out his days in a monastery.

This marked not only the practical end of Merovingian rule but also the establishment of the Carolingian Dynasty. Pepin made efforts to further ingratiate himself with the Catholic Church, intervening on behalf of the pope when Lombardy made threats against Roman territory. He then went a step further and granted the pontiff a generous tract of land in central Italy in 756. This so-called "Donation of Pepin" formed the basis of the Papal States and cemented the relationship between the Frankish kings and the papacy.

Pepin the Short's reign from 751 to 768 was characterized by efforts to consolidate and expand the Frankish Kingdom.

Engaging in campaigns against Germanic tribes, Pepin also played a crucial role in defending the Papal States against Lombard threats. His death in 768 led to, once again, the division of the kingdom between his two sons, Charles and Carloman. However, history seems to have a funny way of rhyming, and much like his great-uncle Carloman, Charles' brother of the same name was not long for his throne. When Carloman died in 771, Charles annexed all his brother's territories–but this was just the beginning of his rise in status. Charles is now known in history by a far more famous name: Charlemagne. His reign marked a period of cultural and political resurgence known as the Carolingian Renaissance, leaving an enduring legacy that would shape the destiny of Western Europe for centuries to come.

5

FRANCIA TO FRANCE AND THE RISE OF THE HOUSE OF CAPET (771–1099 CE)

C arloman's death in 771 saved the Frankish kingdoms from a potentially bloody and protracted civil war. With his brother out of the way, all Charlemagne had to do was disinherit his nephews, and the kingdom was reunited under his hand. Yet, this warrior-king was not satisfied with the borders of his father's accomplishments. He dreamed of more, and under his leadership, power was consolidated in a way not seen since the days of Rome.

Charlemagne, also known as Charles the Great, was likely born around 747. The eldest son of Pepin (Pippin) the Short and his wife, Bertrada (Bertha) of Laon, his early life unfolded against the dynamic backdrop of the Carolingian Dynasty, and his name and upbringing reflected all the prominence that the family had gained under the achievements of his grandfather, Charles Martel.

Growing up in the Frankish court, young Charlemagne received an education that exposed him to the intellectual currents of the time. Despite the turmoil of the period and the dissolution of the Merovingian monarchy, Charlemagne's family managed to consolidate power through strategic alliances and military prowess. His father Pepin's alliance with the Church, marked by the anointing first by Archbishop Boniface and later Pope Stephen II, set a precedent that would shape Charlemagne's own relationship with ecclesiastical authorities. Charlemagne was present for at least the second anointing—his father insisted that both he and his brother Carloman be anointed alongside him as King of the Franks in 754 when the two were merely young boys.

Charlemagne's early experiences were also influenced by the shifting political landscape of Europe. As his father undertook campaigns to expand and solidify the Frankish Kingdom, Charlemagne, even in his youth, was exposed to the complexities of governance and warfare. As mentioned in the previous chapter, upon the death of Pepin in 768, Charlemagne, along with his younger brother Carloman, inherited the Frankish throne. However, their relationship was marred by tensions and conflicts—when a rebellion broke out in Aquitaine, Carloman refused to support Charlemagne's efforts to suppress it. When Carloman passed in 771, it was with relish that Charlemagne annexed his brother's lands.

The work of his Merovingian predecessors, as well as the conquests executed by his father and grandfather, had left Charlemagne in charge of a wide swath of territory inhabited by a diverse group of people. He inherited a legacy of conquest and success via warfare, and it was somewhat of a given that he would rule similarly. Eager to consolidate his power after the death of his brother, Charlemagne embarked on a series of military campaigns that would unite an impressive amount of land and people under his crown.

Finally, thanks to the relationship with the Church secured by his father, Charlemagne was seen as a king by divine right. This was an important consideration: since he was the monarch of many linguistic, cultural, and social groups, one of the main things that tied them all together was their shared Christian faith. Charlemagne's perceived support from God himself lent him a large amount of credibility among all Christians, especially when the advancement of Islamic power from the east tore at the disintegrating Byzantine Empire.

Luckily, Charlemagne had the force of personality to hold up all these great expectations. He is recorded in history as a personable yet formidable man with a strong will, exceptional intellect, and great loyalty to friends and family alike. He had four or five wives, a few mistresses, and eighteen recorded children over whom he personally saw to their development and education. He was a worthy leader and someone who was easy to like and follow.

And indeed, people did follow. Over the next several decades, Charlemagne embarked on a series of ambitious and far-reaching military campaigns that greatly added to his dominion. Ironically enough, his first endeavor ended up being the longest-lasting. The Saxon Wars, unfolding from 772 to 804, were a prolonged series of military campaigns orchestrated by Charlemagne against the Saxons, a Germanic tribe residing in the territory corresponding to present-day Germany. This protracted conflict aimed not only to subdue the Saxons but also to integrate them into the expanding Carolingian Empire, with a parallel objective of spreading Christianity in the region, a goal that had been expressed by both Charles Martel and Pepin the Short. The narrative of the Saxon Wars can be delineated into distinct phases, each contributing to the eventual political and religious assimilation of the Saxons.

In 772, a church was destroyed in Saxon territory by those who wished to preserve their traditional religious customs. Charlemagne responded to this with a punitive expedition, ransacking the Saxon stronghold of Eresburg (inside present-day Marsberg). Housed within Eresburg was a significant cache of treasure as well as the Irminsul, a sacred pillar that had religious, military, social, and political significance to the Saxon people. Charlemagne and his troops desecrated the Irminsul, raided the treasury, and made off with several prisoners of war that Charlemagne hoped to use as collateral to keep the Saxons in line.

However, two years later, the Saxons, now led by a charismatic man named Widukind, began a series of guerrilla raids on Frankish territory, forcing Charlemagne to march back to the region and defeat them in battle in 775. However, Widukind and the Saxons continued to present a problem to Charlemagne, and the conflict steadily escalated, with Charlemagne beginning to demand forced conversions and baptisms of Saxon leaders.

By 782, Widukind was still skirmishing along the Frankish border, killing villagers and burning churches. Charlemagne, ready to be done with this once and for all, ordered a massacre at Verden in Lower Saxony. Roughly 4,500 Saxons were murdered, and Charlemagne subsequently released the

Ordinances Concerning Saxony (Saxon Capitularies), which made the practice of Germanic pagan rituals punishable by death. Three years later, likely ground down by Charlemagne's persistent belligerence against the Saxon people, Widukind appeared before Charlemagne and allowed himself to be baptized, marking a significant shift towards greater integration with the Franks and increased Christianization efforts.

It was quiet in Saxony for a time with Widukind baptized, but in 792, a faction of Saxons rebelled once more, this time in Westphalia. Though Charlemagne managed to stamp it out, the unrest continued throughout the decade, with a new pocket of agitation appearing as soon as another had been extinguished. Charlemagne attempted to soften his treatment of the Saxons, hoping to win them over. He removed the death penalty on pagan practices and stopped forced conversions and baptisms toward the end of the eighth century, but this still proved unsuccessful in furthering his goal to subdue and rule Saxony. Finally, in 804, the Saxon Wars were ended by deporting ten thousand Saxons to the Frankish region of Neustria and moving a considerable number of Frankish settlers into Saxon lands. This forced assimilation sped up the process of Christianization and made Saxon unity nigh impossible, taking the teeth out of any further Saxon uprisings.

In between his forays into Saxony, Charlemagne also worked to expand his kingdom to the south, particularly in a region called Lombardy—a portion of land in northern Italy. In 770, prior to his brother's death, Charlemagne entered an arranged marriage with Desiderata, the daughter of the Lombard King Desiderius, to create a closer bond between the kingdoms of Francia and Lombardy. However, it appears this relationship was an unhappy one. Whether he genuinely did not care for Desiderata and the Lombards or if they simply stood in the way of his expansionary plans is unknown. Still, soon after becoming the sole king of Francia in 771, he broke off the marriage and renounced his alliance with King Desiderius.

Shortly afterward, in 773, Charlemagne embarked on a significant military campaign in Lombardy, a strategic move aimed at asserting Frankish control over the Lombard Kingdom. This campaign marked a crucial chapter in Charlemagne's efforts to expand the Carolingian Empire and solidify his influence in the Italian Peninsula.

Charlemagne's decision to intervene in Lombardy was prompted by King Desiderius' perceived aggressions against the Papal States and the city of Rome. Faced with the prospect of a hostile neighbor in Italy, Charlemagne deemed it imperative to curb Lombard ambitions and secure the interests of the Frankish Kingdom.

The campaign unfolded throughout 773 and into 774 as Charlemagne led his forces across the Alps into Lombardy. The Frankish army, known for its disciplined and organized structure, confronted the Lombard forces in a series of engagements. The decisive moment came in 774 when Charlemagne emerged victorious, leading to the capture of King Desiderius. With the Lombard Kingdom subdued, Charlemagne assumed the title "King of the Franks and the Lombards," signaling the establishment of Frankish dominance in Italy. This victory not only secured the safety of the Papal States but also enhanced Charlemagne's reputation as a formidable ruler in Western Europe and a defender of the papacy and the Catholic Church.

Charlemagne's presence in Italy had broader implications for the political landscape of the region. His conquest of Lombardy and subsequent adoption of the Lombards' crown marked a crucial step toward the unification of disparate territories under the Carolingian Empire. Furthermore, Charlemagne's positive interactions with the papacy set the stage for a fruitful relationship. This connection with the pope would ultimately lead to a momentous event that would come to redefine the relationship between temporal and spiritual authority in medieval Europe.

In Charlemagne's mind, the subjugation of Lombardy and Saxony was not enough to secure his kingdom's borders. He was leery of the threat to the southwest that had haunted his grandfather, Charles Martel. The Umayyad Caliphate still ruled in Spain, and Charlemagne felt compelled to do something about the Muslim influence in the region.

In 778, Charlemagne embarked on an expedition to the Iberian Peninsula, aimed at aiding the Christian Kingdom of Asturias in the north of the peninsula against the Umayyad Caliphate. Marching his army south through the Pyrenees, Charlemagne was prepared to fight as always, but the circumstances and outcomes of the campaign proved more complex than initially anticipated. Instead of the Franks proving victorious, Charlemagne and his armies were forced to retreat. While doing so, they were ambushed by a troop of Gascon (Basque) forces. This fierce battle at Roncevaux Pass, a mountainous route in the Pyrenees, led to the death of most of Charlemagne's rearguard, including their leader, a knight named Roland. Though Charlemagne and the bulk of his army moved through the pass unscathed, the Gascon soldiers attacked the final portion of the Frankish army and exacted a terrible toll. The events at Roncevaux Pass would later be romanticized in the medieval epic poem, *The Song of Roland.*

The campaign in Spain did not lead to lasting territorial gains for Charlemagne in the region. Instead, it highlighted the complex geopolitical dynamics of the time, with Christian kingdoms in the Iberian Peninsula seeking external support against Muslim rule. However, Charlemagne's involvement demonstrated his role as a Christian leader willing to defend Christian territories beyond his own realm. It contributed to his reputation as a defender of Christendom and a leader willing to risk his nation's military for other people.

No border of Charlemagne's lands remained unexplored. His consistent military action led him and his armies all over Europe, and the 790s saw him moving to the east against the Avar people. Nomads hailing from the Eurasian Steppes, the Avars migrated westward and established a formidable nomadic state around the mid-500s CE known as the Avar Khaganate. Located in the Carpathian Basin, which includes parts of present-day Hungary, Austria, Slovakia, and Romania, the Avar Khaganate was mostly known for its strategic location and military prowess. This strength looming on his eastern border posed a daunting challenge to the stability of Charlemagne's realm. Eager to neutralize this potential threat and extend Frankish influence, Charlemagne engaged the Avars in battle.

Charlemagne's campaign against the Avars waged between 791 and 796. It was a series of entanglements aimed at subduing the Avar Khaganate, which employed a combination of military force and strategic diplomacy. His armies attacked the Avars in a series of sieges, skirmishes, and maneuvers across the Carpathian Basin.

One focal point of Charlemagne's strategy was the destruction of the Avar Ring, a system of defensive fortifications that had neatly deterred previous invaders. Charlemagne's forces, however, systematically dismantled these strongholds and weakened the Avar Khaganate's defensive capabilities. Regarding diplomacy, Charlemagne sought alliances with neighboring peoples, encouraging some Avar nobles to switch allegiances and join his cause, gradually eroding Avar power. By 796, Charlemagne prevailed over the Avars, incorporating much of their territory into his Carolingian Empire.

By the end of the eighth century, Charlemagne's Frankish kingdom was the preeminent power of the West. He had also molded himself as the chief defender of the Christian faith against all other entities, Muslim and pagan alike. The culmination of all these achievements arrived on December 25, 800, when Charlemagne was crowned as the Holy Roman Emperor by Pope Leo III in Rome. One crucial element was the imperative to safeguard the Papal States, which, as mentioned above, had faced external threats in Italy over the last century. The coronation further signified an intensification in the strategic alliance between Charlemagne and the papacy, offering reciprocal protection and support.

The act also held profound historical and symbolic implications. The title "Holy Roman Emperor" revived the idea of a Western Roman Empire, with Charlemagne seen as its legitimate successor. This gesture aimed to establish a connection between the ancient Roman legacy and the emerging Carolingian Empire.

Beyond symbolism, the coronation served to legitimize Charlemagne's authority. Ruling over a vast and diverse empire, he needed divine validation for his power. The imperial coronation provided a sacred dimension, portraying his rule as sanctioned by God, thereby adding increased legitimacy to his governance as a Christian ruler.

The crowning of Charlemagne also symbolized a new unity for Christendom. By uniting the spiritual authority of the Pope with the temporal power of the Holy Roman Emperor, the event conveyed the vision of a Christian empire transcending regional, cultural, and ethnic divisions. This coronation was a landmark moment in European history, encapsulating the fusion of political and religious authority.

After 800, Charlemagne's remarkable achievements and contributions to the Carolingian Empire continued unabated. His adept leadership introduced a system of governance that divided the empire into administrative units referred to by the familiar term "counties." Each region, in turn, was overseen by loyal nobles or counts, facilitating efficient management and governance across his many diverse territories. His desire for order and uniformity extended into his legal actions. He issued multiple "capitularies" or legislative acts that covered a spectrum of governance, addressing legal, economic, and ecclesiastical matters. It was important to Charlemagne that his diverse and vast territories all behaved as one empire in word as well as in deed.

Additionally, his close alliance with the Church was integral to his rule, and he was deeply aware of the significance that his religious legitimacy held. He collaborated closely with the papacy, actively supported the spread of Christianity within his territories, and strengthened the Church's influence over Europe. This synergy of the ecclesiastical and temporal authorities of the West contributed to a broader cultural and educational revival known to history as the Carolingian Renaissance.

Spanning the reign of Charlemagne and the subsequent Carolingian rulers of the late eighth and ninth centuries, the Carolingian Renaissance saw a resurgence of learning, arts, and classical scholarship. This all began with Charlemagne, who, recognizing the importance of education and cultural refinement, actively promoted a culture of learning within his court. He attracted scholars and thinkers from across Europe, creating a vibrant intellectual center. One of the notable achievements of the Carolingian Renaissance was the preservation and copying of classical texts, including the works of Cicero, Horace, and Julius Caesar. Monastic scriptoria, or writing rooms, were established where monks meticulously copied these ancient manuscripts, safeguarding the knowledge of antiquity for future generations.

In addition to preserving classical knowledge, the Carolingian scholars also created new works. This intellectual activity was not limited to religious subjects but extended to various fields, including grammar, rhetoric, astronomy, and philosophy. Alcuin of York, a prominent scholar in Charlemagne's court from the British Isles, played a pivotal role in shaping the intellectual landscape of the Carolingian Renaissance. As the head of the Palatine School founded by Charlemagne in Aachen, he brought the humanistic ideas espoused by the Anglo-Saxons as well as English educational methods to the school where many prominent Franks were educated, including Charlemagne and his sons.

Continuing in the field of education, Charlemagne aimed to improve literacy among the clerical and noble classes. The establishment of a standardized script, known as the Carolingian minuscule, facilitated easier reading and writing, contributing to the overall proliferation of literacy in Charlemagne's realm.

Art and architecture remain as testaments to the Carolingian Renaissance, as well. Monasteries and churches were built or renovated in a style that blended classical elements with Germanic and Christian motifs. The Palatine Chapel in Aachen[6] and the gatehouse of the monastery at Lorsch[7] stand as examples of the unique blend that Carolingian architecture offered. Beyond buildings, illuminated manuscripts characterized by intricate illustrations and ornate decorations became iconic expressions of Carolingian artistic achievements. The Drogo Sacramentary[8] from around 850 is a beautiful example of this kind of artistry.

While the Carolingian Renaissance did not achieve the same level of cultural and intellectual sophistication as the Italian Renaissance that followed in later centuries, it laid the groundwork for the preservation and transmission of classical knowledge. The cultural and educational revival initiated during this period contributed to the shaping of medieval European intellectual traditions and left a lasting impact on the foundations of Western civilization.

Despite all this civilized growth and enlightenment, persistent military challenges continued to rear their heads. Thus, Charlemagne remained engaged in campaigns to defend and expand his realm. His military endeavors included campaigns against the Moors in Spain and skirmishes with the Slavs in Eastern Europe.

However, like all men, Charlemagne's time on earth was fleeting. To ensure the future of his empire, he took a significant step in 813. This act associated his son, Louis, with the imperial title, hoping to secure a smooth transition of power and establish a clear line of succession within the Carolingian Empire. With this, Charlemagne signaled his intent for Louis to inherit both the Carolingian legacy and all the responsibilities that came with ruling the vast empire.

Upon Charlemagne's death in 814, the Carolingian Empire was at its territorial height, reaching from the Atlantic Ocean in the west and incorporating modern-day France, Belgium, Luxembourg, and part of the Netherlands. To the north, it extended into modern-day Germany, including territories east of the Rhine River, and butted up against Slavic territories. The eastern borders of the Carolingian Empire snaked into territories that are now part of Switzerland, Austria, and bits of the Czech Republic. It was Charlemagne's campaigns against the Avars in the late eighth century that contributed to the expansion of the empire into Eastern Europe, though the Avars still held land in that region. To the southeast, Charlemagne's rule extended into Lombardy and central portions of the Italian peninsula while also sharing a border with the Umayyad Caliphate of Córdoba near the Pyrenees Mountains.

All this passed on to Louis, as decreed by Charlemagne, who ascended to the throne shortly after his father's passing. Louis, often referred to as Louis the Pious or Louis I, faced the challenge of maintaining the unity of the empire and upholding the Carolingian legacy without the tour de force of his father's personality. His reign involved efforts to consolidate power, address internal challenges, and contend with external threats to the empire.

While Charlemagne's vision of a hereditary monarchy had been realized with the ascension of his son, the following decades saw complexities in the succession process, including conflicts among Louis's sons. The subsequent period witnessed power struggles and divisions within the Carolingian Empire, which will be discussed momentarily.

Louis the Pious, after inheriting the esteemed title of Holy Roman Emperor from his illustrious father, reigned from 814 to 840. At the onset of his rule, Louis aimed to reform and strengthen his father's vision for a united empire. He leaned on religion to do so, seeing himself as the temporal emperor of the Christian people rather than the leader of any one cultural or ethnic group. In 817, Louis aimed to further bolster the administrative and governmental strength of the Carolingian Empire by attempting to clearly define the roles that each of his sons were to have in the future of his kingdom. This ruling, known as the *Ordinatio imperii,* made his eldest son, Lothar (Lothair), co-emperor with him while assigning his younger sons Pepin (Pippin) and Louis (the German) kingships of the regions of

Aquitaine and Bavaria, respectively. With this arrangement, Pepin and Louis the German fell under the authority of their father and their eldest brother, Lothar.

As a result of his attention to religion, Louis's reign was characterized by his noteworthy piety. Building upon Charlemagne's legacy of supporting the Church, he embarked on a series of ecclesiastical reforms. He pushed for the spread of Christianity throughout Europe. However, the fabric of unity began to unravel as internal strife gripped Louis's family during his later years. When another son, Charles the Bald, was born in 823 to Louis' second wife, the issue of inheritance between the sons became disruptive to the empire. Disputes among his children over inheritance rights and conflicting loyalties erupted into open rebellion by the 830s, with Louis' three eldest sons attempting a coup against their father in hopes of "freeing" him from the clutches of his second wife.

This ultimately failed and led to the issuance of the *Divisio regnorum*, which replaced the *Ordinatio imperiii*. Essentially, this followed the traditional Frankish practice of dividing inheritance evenly amongst one's sons, and the Carolingian Empire was split into four equal territories that were slated to become independent kingdoms upon the death of Louis the Pious. The once-cohesive Carolingian Empire faced internal discord, significantly compromising its unity and stability, with many factions supporting the continued unity of the Carolingian Empire in direct conflict with the new *Divisio regnorum*. One of Louis' sons, Pepin, died in 838, and he further inflamed his sons' agitation when he refused to grant Pepin's holdings in Aquitaine to Pepin's son and his grandson. Instead, he handed the territory over to his youngest child, Charles. When Louis passed in 840, a civil war between his offspring ensued.

This war spanned the years 840 to 843. It centered around an inheritance dispute between Louis' three surviving sons: Lothar, Louis the German, and Charles the Bald. Each vied for a significant share of the empire, leading to a complex web of alliances, entanglements, violence, and revolts.

The discord between the brothers escalated into a series of armed confrontations that were marred by needless death and destruction. One of the pivotal clashes occurred at the Battle of Fontenoy in 841, in the north-central region of present-day France, between the forces of Lothar and his nephew Pepin II and the allied forces of Louis the German and Charles the Bald. Not much is known regarding the number of casualties or troops involved, but the combined forces of Lothar and Pepin II were defeated. Lothar retreated, but the conflict between the sons of Louis continued.

Amid the ongoing strife, the brothers and their respective factions engaged in negotiations that culminated in the signing of the Treaty of Verdun in 843. This agreement divided the Carolingian Empire into three sections along a north-south axis. Lothar retained the imperial title granted to his father and grandfather, but the impact of that accolade had eroded over the years. The three new kingdoms were christened Francia Orientalis, Francia Media, and Francia Occidentalis, and each of the three brothers was viewed as equal in both rank and territory. Francia Orientalis, or East Francia, went to Louis the German and became the foundation for the later Kingdom of Germany and the Holy Roman

Empire. Francia Media, or Middle Francia, was ruled by Lothar. It turned out to be the most unstable of the three kingdoms, and it was ultimately divided between East and West Francia following Lothar's death. Francia Occidentalis, or West Francia, was awarded to Charles the Bald and formed the basis for the Kingdom of France.

The primary objective of the Treaty of Verdun was to bring clarity to the inheritance disputes and establish stable territorial boundaries for Louis the Pious's grandsons. However, the consequences of this division were far-reaching, shaping the medieval political landscape. While providing a temporary resolution to internal strife, the treaty set the stage for the emergence of distinct European kingdoms. In retrospect, the Treaty of Verdun played a pivotal role in delineating the territories that would form the foundation for modern nations.

The realm of West Francia was beset by challenges both at home and abroad. Peace seemed a foreign concept, and beginning with Charles the Bald, it appeared that none of the subsequent Carolingian rulers of the kingdom could provide stability for their subjects. Hierarchies broke down internally, and poor lines of communication led to lesser nobles taking on more regional power in an attempt to protect vulnerable villages and outposts that the crown seemed unable or unwilling to defend. This lack of support and growth of regional control assisted in the gradual erosion of royal authority.

Magyars, an ethnic group native to present-day Hungary, threatened the kingdom from the east, while Muslim forces in the Mediterranean proved a problem to the south.

However, the most serious issue for West Francia was the Viking warriors descending from the north. The Vikings raided and pillaged various parts of West Francia, including its coastlines and inland areas. Charles had to contend with the defense of his realm against these relentless Norse incursions.

Mostly seeking gold and other treasures in their raids, the Vikings could sometimes be bribed away with valuables. However, there were times when nothing would keep these raiders out. Throughout the latter half of the ninth century, Norse interlopers struck Paris multiple times, as well as smaller settlements and towns like Bordeaux, Toulouse, Orléans, Reims, and Soissons. This slowed down during the final decades of the 800s as many Vikings began establishing more permanent settlements in the Seine Valley. From there, they gradually spread westward, contributing to the formation of Normandy.

Again, local lords and nobles were able to profit from these crises, using them to enrich their lands and titles. Throughout the 900s and 1000s, West Francia devolved into a veritable patchwork of lordships, duchies, and fiefdoms, though still nominally under the rule of a monarch. At first, this king was a member of the Carolingian dynasty, but towards the end of the 900s, a change in leadership was underway.

The Carolingian family managed to hold on to power for another hundred years or so after the Treaty of Verdun. The main power of the king of West Francia was centered around the city of Paris. Due to fragmentation over the years, many smaller sub-kingdoms had arisen, like Burgundy, Anjou,

Brittany, Normandy, and others. In 987, the last Carolingian King, Louis V, or Louis the Sluggard, died childless. The Frankish nobles decided to elect a powerful duke, Hugh Capet, to the position of king, becoming the first non-Carolingian king of West Francia.

Born in 938 to Hugh the Great and Hedwig of Saxony, Hugh Capet had an impressive estate to his name, including tracts of land around Paris and Orléans. This influence, coupled with the fact that the only legitimate surviving Carolingian heir, Charles of Lorraine, was unpopular, made Hugh Capet's election possible. However, it should be noted that it was not some incredible departure from tradition. To be sure, the monarchy mainly had been inherited through the direct Carolingian line since Pepin the Short, but there were exceptions here and there, including the brief kingship of Hugh Capet's grandfather, Robert I, from 922 to 923. Furthermore, Hugh Capet was a wealthy man from a connected family that had genetic ties to the Carolingian line. So, though unprecedented, it was not a subversive move on the part of the Frankish nobles.

As the founder of the Capetian line that would go on to rule France for centuries as well as spawn the cadet branches of the House of Valois and House of Bourbon, one would assume that Hugh Capet was a formidable character like Charlemagne or a consequential historical figure like Clovis. However, this is not quite the case. Hugh's reign was plagued by continual attempts by others, notably the would-be Carolingian heir Charles of Lorraine, to seize his throne.

Conspiracies abounded like fleas on a dog, and historians note that the only reason Hugh likely survived and managed to ensure his son's succession was due to the failure of his enemies, not to any great strategy or success on his part. Nevertheless, Hugh Capet did start one tradition that secured his dynasty's longevity and stability: he crowned his son and successor, Robert II, before his death. This custom continued through all the Capetian kings until the late 1100s.

Hugh's authority was centralized around Île-de-France, a region in north-central West Francia, home to the city of Paris. Local dukes and nobles outside this area continued to exert an outsized amount of control. The kingdom remained largely decentralized, although Hugh did manage to secure political alliances, like his marriage to Adelaide of Aquitaine, the daughter of the Duke of Aquitaine. As an aside, though it was not until 1190 that the name "France" was used for the former kingdom of West Francia, moving forward, the text will utilize the term France. The use of the term "West Francia" largely fell out of favor in the historical record following the election of Hugh Capet.

For clarity, we will now briefly discuss some of the major powerbrokers in France outside of the Île-de-France region. Flanders, Normandy, Blois-Champagne, Anjou, Brittany, and Burgundy were to the north. Flanders, now a primarily Dutch-speaking region in northern Belgium, was ruled over by a series of particularly audacious counts descended from Baldwin I, the first Count of Flanders, in the mid-800s. The region became known for trade and was home to the prosperous city of Ghent. As mentioned earlier, Normandy was home to a group of Viking settlers led by the chieftain Rollo (Hrolf), who were granted the land by the Carolingian King Charles III (the Simple) in 911. This mostly included land around the present-day towns of Evreux and Rouen. The history of Normandy is somewhat muddy, but in 1066, their duke, William II (the Conqueror), took control of England after establishing his strength and power in his home of Normandy. Becoming the king of England made him one of, if not the, most powerful ruler in France at the time.

To the east, Blois-Champagne was ruled by a series of counts who posed a serious threat to royal power, especially due to its geographical proximity to Paris. Anjou, in the lower Loire Valley south of Paris, did not have the strength that other principalities surrounding Paris wielded. Like Blois-Champagne and Flanders, it was also ruled over by a string of counts who were frequently landholders elsewhere, like Henry II of England, the founder of the Angevin dynasty, and the Duke of Normandy and Count of Anjou.

Even further to the west than Anjou and Normandy, Brittany remained a stronghold of Celtic culture. Even today, the Breton language, a Gaelic tongue, lives on in the region. Established as a duchy during the tenth century, it later became part of England under the rule of King Henry II of England during the twelfth century. Finally, Burgundy, to the east of Paris and south of Blois-Champagne, began as a powerful duchy in its own right, repelling both Magyar and Viking invaders alike, but it was later absorbed into the royal portfolio, becoming the property of the Capetian family. It should also be noted that Burgundy was also the name of a kingdom in the region, though this is separate from the duchy.

South of the Loire River remained just as fractured as the north. The territories of Auvergne, Provence, Toulouse,

Barcelona, and Aquitaine exercised considerable power during the ninth, tenth, and eleventh centuries. Auvergne, a region in south-central France named for Vercingetorix's Arverni tribe, became a region of factious discord. It never truly coalesced under any one power, and it was ultimately absorbed by the French crown in the 1200s.

As for Provence, it was passed around from power to power. Now in the southeastern corner of present-day France, it was not initially a part of France. Instead, it fell under the auspices of Middle Francia, though this was a short-lived political entity. Instead, Provence was controlled at various times by Burgundian kings, but smaller local counts were called upon to defend the territory against interloping Muslim raiders in the Mediterranean. However, these local nobles lost out when Provence was eventually split between Toulouse and Barcelona during the 1100s.

Toulouse, though a formidable Frankish power during the 700s and a noble holding since the early 900s, was unable to establish any kind of dynastic continuity. It was continually skirmishing with neighboring duchies, namely Barcelona and Aquitaine. It never managed to accrue a significant amount of power or influence. On the other hand, Barcelona managed to become largely independent, forming one of the most powerful principalities in the south. It remained nominally under the control of the French kings until 1258, when the Treaty of Corbeil separated Barcelona from the political entities of southern France.

Aquitaine, powerful like Barcelona, had been its own kingdom in the 800s and became an influential duchy in the early 1000s under William V, Duke of Aquitaine. Though regularly in conflict with the various Angevin counts to the north, Aquitaine was coveted by kings and nobles alike. During the twelfth century, one of its most famous heiresses, Eleanor of Aquitaine, brought her vast duchy with her as a prize for her marriages to both the kings of France and England.

In 1137, she wed Louis VII of France, becoming the Queen of France and binding Aquitaine to the French crown. However, after a fifteen-year marriage and two daughters, the couple grew apart, and an annulment was granted in 1152 since no son had been produced. Aquitaine became solely hers again with the dissolution of her first marriage, but just two months later, she wed once more, this time to a young Henry Plantagenet, the Count of Anjou and the Duke of Normandy.

Two years later, Henry Plantagenet became Henry II of England, and Aquitaine was bound to the English crown until the conclusion of the Hundred Years' War in 1453. Eleanor and Henry had five sons and three daughters, two of whom—Richard I (the Lionheart) and John—went on to become kings of England. Thanks to her marriages, children, and familial connections, Eleanor is sometimes called the "grandmother of Europe." Beyond that, she was a canny and wise woman who contributed significantly to the kingdoms she ruled. After Henry II died in 1189, she continued to assist both her sons in their reigns until she retired to a monastery in Anjou in 1202. Now in her eighties, she lived out her remaining two years among nuns who remembered her in her obituary as a queen "who surpassed almost all the queens in the world."

As evidenced by the numerous duchies and territories outlined above, life in West Francia was heavily fractured and localized at this time. The idea of centralized authority coming from the king was not yet established. Instead, the common folk relied on the protection and guidance of their local lord, count, duke, or other member of the nobility. This worked well for the nobility, who sought autonomy and eagerly adopted a pivotal role in the ever-evolving landscape. The social system that outlined this form of hierarchy was called feudalism, and the economic system that accompanied it became known as manorialism.

Feudalism, a complex web of reciprocal relationships between lords and vassals, quickly became the prevailing social order. Lords bestowed parcels of land, known as fiefs, upon vassals in exchange for military service and loyalty. This hierarchy created a framework for the distribution of power and resources, where fealty was the currency of governance.

Simultaneously, an economic system that went hand-in-hand with this social order arose: manorialism. The manor, a self-sufficient estate, became the nucleus of medieval life. Comprising the lord's residence, farmlands, villages, and common lands, the manor fostered an interdependent community. Serfs—peasants tethered to the land—toiled in the fields, providing labor in exchange for protection and the privilege of cultivating a portion of the land for sustenance. The need for local defense against invasions, such as Viking raids, played a crucial role in the genesis of these systems.

In the vacuum left by the weakened central authority, the Church wielded strong influence, endorsing the divine hierarchy that justified the rule of kings and the protective role of lords. Socially stratified, the medieval hierarchy placed kings and monarchs at the zenith, followed by nobles, vassals, and then peasants. Within this framework, the majority of the populace were peasants, including both serfs and free peasants, each occupying a designated rung on the societal ladder.

Yet despite these systems becoming the socially acceptable and religiously endorsed way of life, urban areas were the birthplace of the initial resistance against feudal and manorial dominance. These areas, called communes, were frequently in an urban center, though there is some evidence of rural areas organizing themselves into a commune-like entity. No one commune was exactly like the other, but it usually started with some kind of charter or oath that bound the citizens of the town into an agreement that assured the inhabitants would protect and help one another when necessary. Yet, despite their contrast to feudalism, these were not bastions of democracy or popular rule. Usually, an oligarchic system was in place for governance, placing the wealthy and well-connected above the others in the town. They were similar to the city-states of Italy, and a solid example of a commune from the era is the town of Ghent in Flanders.

Aside from the manor systems and the communes, France had a proliferation of religious communities at the time. Monasteries, which became homes to monks and nuns alike, also became a bulwark of learning, artistry, and culture, particularly of the popular medieval art of manuscript illumination[9]. Some of these abbeys, like Mont-Saint-Michel[10] in Normandy, became examples of architectural artistry as well. Construction on the famed Romanesque church at the abbey of Mont-Saint-Michel began during the eleventh century, though the site had been religiously significant in the area since the 700s.

The abbey at Cluny also became an incredibly important institution during the tenth and eleventh centuries, shaping the direction of monastic life for the remainder of the medieval period. Nestled in the picturesque town of Cluny, Saône-et-Loire, France, Cluny Abbey[11], founded in 910 by Duke William I of Aquitaine, rose to prominence as a pivotal Benedictine monastery during the Middle Ages. Guided by the visionary leadership of its first abbot, Berno of Baume (Berno of Cluny), the abbey embarked on a mission of monastic reform, emphasizing a return to the strictures of the Rule of St. Benedict. This reform movement, known as the Cluniac Reforms, sought to elevate the spiritual rigor of Benedictine communities.

Over the centuries, Cluny Abbey underwent remarkable expansions and renovations, with the crowning achievement being the construction of Cluny III in the late eleventh century. This architectural masterpiece, representing the zenith of Romanesque design, solidified Cluny's status as one of the largest Christian edifices in medieval Europe.

Beyond its architectural splendor, Cluny became a beacon of intellectual pursuits, scholarship, and artistic endeavors. The abbey's scriptorium flourished, producing illuminated manuscripts that played a crucial role in preserving and transmitting classical knowledge. Cluny's monks were renowned for their unwavering commitment to liturgical practices, making the abbey a vibrant religious center. With vast landholdings and economic influence, Cluny Abbey transcended its religious role, emerging as a significant political force in medieval Europe. The abbey's wealth and privileges granted by papal decrees afforded it a degree of independence from secular authorities, including kings.

The importance of religious life at this time in Europe in general and France in particular is highlighted by the culture's choice of artistic expression. The finest examples of architecture were churches and monasteries, and the most beautiful examples of visual art are illuminated manuscripts of holy texts or paintings depicting religious themes and scenes. Christian religion was central to daily life and influenced social, political, and military choices made by individuals of both common and noble birth. These choices could be inconsequential or devastating, depending on the circumstances and the outcome.

One such choice would be the Crusades, a series of religious wars fought during the medieval era with the express goal of retaking the Holy Land of Jerusalem and its surrounding areas from the Islamic rule of the Seljuk and Fatimid empires. On November 27, 1095, Pope Urban II gave an impassioned speech at the Council of Clermont in central France, urging the recapture of Jerusalem for Christendom. He promised that those who fought on behalf of Christianity would be granted an indulgence: their sins would be wholly forgiven pending their military service in the Holy Land.

Urban II's urgings were heeded the following year, and the First Crusade commenced. Propelled by a blend of religious zeal and geopolitical considerations, Urban II's answer came not only from the organized forces of knights and nobles but also from common people who marched toward the Holy

Land with ardor. The best example of this would be Peter the Hermit, a charismatic and zealous priest. Leading the People's Crusade, a popular movement preceding the main Crusader armies, he inspired a diverse and unorganized group of followers, including peasants and commoners, to embark on a journey to liberate Jerusalem. Despite his initial impact, Peter's movement faced numerous challenges, and its uncoordinated nature led to difficulties during the march to the Holy Land. Nevertheless, the bulk of the forces, both organized and unorganized, hailed from France, but other European entities joined in as well.

There were many hardships on the road to Jerusalem, including hunger, disease, and infighting, but when the first battle came at the Siege of Nicaea in present-day Türkiye in 1097, the Crusaders were victorious. After leaving Nicaea in June, the Crusaders met with the Seljuk forces again at Dorylaeum in July, a site near the modern-day city of Eskişehir in Türkiye. Once again, the European forces claimed victory over the Seljuks, continuing their march southward toward Jerusalem and what they saw as their destiny.

However, before they reached the Holy Land, they engaged in a protracted and grueling siege at Antioch in what is now the town of Antaka in southern Türkiye. It began in October of 1097 and did not conclude until June 1098, when the city finally fell to the Crusaders. After taking much-needed time to recover, the European forces marched for Jerusalem at long last, reaching the Holy City in June 1099.

Naturally, the city did not fall without a fight, and the Siege of Jerusalem began shortly after the Crusaders' arrival, with weeks of intense struggle. At last, the Europeans breached the city walls on July 15, 1099. The capture of Jerusalem heralded the establishment of Crusader states in the region, including the Kingdom of Jerusalem, the County of Edessa, the Principality of Antioch, and the County of Tripoli. The First Crusade became a defining moment in the interaction between Christians and Muslims, shaping the course of the medieval world.

France, with its powerful nobles and deep connection to the Catholic Church, was now well and truly on its way to becoming the recognizable entity it is known as today. As the eleventh century faded into the twelfth, the kingdom was poised to become a major powerbroker in Europe.

6

WAR, PLAGUE, FAMINE, AND DEATH (1100–1475 CE)

A t the beginning of the twelfth century, France was a kingdom with rising power. The outcome of the First Crusade had left most of Christendom on a victory high, sure in their position as the righteous defenders of their one true faith. France was no exception as the chief supplier of men and arms during the fighting. However, the French monarchy was still an essentially nominal power, flexing its authority mainly around Île-de-France and failing to match the might of their ducal rivals, especially those in Flanders and Normandy. This was further compounded by the second marriage of Eleanor of Aquitaine to Henry II of Anjou.

As mentioned in the previous chapter, the prize of Aquitaine had initially fallen to the French crown during Eleanor's first marriage to King Louis VII, but the breakdown of their relationship led Eleanor to wed his chief rival, dealing a sizeable territorial blow to the kingdom of France. Eleanor's inheritance was vast, comprising the rich and expansive region of Aquitaine in southwestern France. This marriage added to

Henry II's already considerable holdings, which included Normandy and Anjou. The combination of these territories laid the foundation for what would later be known as the Angevin Empire.

Aside from the vast holdings on the European continent, Henry II was also the monarch of England, ruling from the Scottish borderlands down to the English Channel and even claiming a portion of eastern Ireland. The addition of French lands to the English crown set off centuries of discord, warfare, and rivalries between the kingdoms of England and France.

Though impressive, the Angevin Empire did not stand for long. Before Henry II's death, the security of Angevin land holdings was already wobbling. A disastrous civil war between the king and his sons had damaged the strength of the English crown. Furthermore, his two elder sons, Henry the Young King and Geoffrey, preceded their father to the grave. So, Henry II's third son, Richard I, "the Lionheart," inherited the throne and managed to keep the empire whole despite his sojourn in the Holy Land during the Third Crusade. This was essentially thanks to his mother's efforts. However, when his younger brother John took the crown after him, he was a weaker ruler and lost much of the land his father had built. Though England continued to control pieces of France throughout the ensuing centuries, it was never as significant as what Henry II had managed to hold.

In the face of instability in England, the kingdom of France was gifted at long last with a strong ruler capable of using the vulnerabilities of his rival to his advantage. Philip II, widely known as Philip Augustus, ascended to the throne of

France at the youthful age of 15 in 1180, succeeding his father, Louis VII, Eleanor of Aquitaine's first husband. Like his predecessors, Philip II was faced with challenges from powerful vassals and internal unrest, but he adeptly navigated these difficulties early in his reign. Philip II's overarching goal was to consolidate the royal domain, reclaiming territories that had been lost in previous reigns. Through a combination of strategic marriages, diplomatic maneuvers, and military campaigns, he successfully recovered key regions and greatly strengthened the power of the French monarchy.

His first marriage to Isabella of Hainault in 1180 brought with it the territory of Artois as part of her dowry. During the tail end of the 1180s, Philip II was able to chip away a small bit of the borderlands of Normandy, and following the death of Henry II in 1189, he was able to lay claim to the majority of Auvergne, though he did not gain true control over the area until 1214.

The absence of King Richard I from the region during the Third Crusade also provided Philip II with an opportunity to strengthen his position in France, but it was not until the reign of King John that Philip II was able to take a significant portion of the Angevin Empire for himself. In 1202, a legal technicality allowed Philip II to neatly seize control of the majority of John's French holdings, claiming that the English king had violated feudal law. Naturally, war ensued. Between 1204 and 1206, Philip II successfully annexed Normandy, Maine, Anjou, and Touraine, leaving only Aquitaine and a few other inconsequential bits of France in English hands. Fighting between the French and English was significant, and what is now known as the Anglo-French War spread beyond the two kingdoms, with the Holy Roman Empire, the County of Flanders, and the County of Boulogne all lending their support to the Angevin Empire. This culminated at the Battle of Bouvines in 1214 when Philip II successfully routed his enemies, defeating the English coalition. The Truce of Chinon in 1214 solidified Philip II's winnings and further recognized his authority over the region of Brittany, though royal authority would take time to be fully established in the area.

Essentially, with the conclusion of Philip II's reign at his death in 1223, the only pieces of France that did not wholly answer to him were Brittany, Flanders, Champagne, Burgundy, Toulouse, and Aquitaine. With such an impressive tract of land to his royal name, Philip II became the first monarch to style himself as the King of France, rather than the previously utilized moniker, the King of the Franks.

Aside from expanding his influence internally, Philip II was also interested in becoming a bigger power player in Europe externally. This troubled his fellow monarchs, but there was no real check on his power aside from the skirmishing of the Anglo-French War. He was now the leader of Europe's most heavily populated area, which lent him outsized access to resources compared to his contemporaries. As a result, he took a more prominent role in the political leanings of Europe, as demonstrated by his involvement with the Third Crusade.

The Holy Land had been retaken by Saladin, the sultan of the Ayyubid dynasty, in 1187. The three most powerful monarchs in Europe at the time—King Richard I, "the Lionheart" of the Angevin Empire, Holy Roman Emperor

Frederick Barbarossa (Frederick I), and, of course, King Philip II of France—banded together to address this loss of Christian power. Their collaboration aimed to set aside political differences and unite in the common cause of liberating Jerusalem.

The German contingent, led by Holy Roman Emperor Frederick Barbarossa, faced a tragic setback when the emperor drowned in the Saleph (Göksu) River in Anatolia in 1190. Despite this loss, the remaining leaders pressed forward with campaigns in the Levant, culminating in capturing the coastal city of Acre in 1191, a significant achievement for the Christian forces. However, internal discord and rivalries among the European leaders surfaced, preventing a unified advance towards Jerusalem. In 1192, Richard the Lionheart and Saladin negotiated the Treaty of Jaffa, a diplomatic accord that granted Christians access to Jerusalem's holy sites without regaining control of the city itself. While the primary objective of reclaiming Jerusalem remained unfulfilled, the crusade's impact endured. The Treaty of Jaffa set a precedent for diplomatic engagements between Crusader states and Muslim powers, shaping the complex dynamics of the Holy Land for years to come.

Once that campaign was set aside, Philip II rarely looked anywhere other than England when it came to his expansionary motivations. After his first wife passed away, he looked for another woman who would provide advantageous connections and found her in Ingeborg of Denmark, the sister to the current king of Denmark. However, Ingeborg and Philip II did not get along in the slightest—he imprisoned her and attempted to either annul their marriage or divorce her for many years. It has been hypothesized that his initial impetus for the union was due to his Danish brother-in-law's distant claim to the English throne. He also wed his son, Louis, to Blanche of Castile, the granddaughter of his old nemesis, Henry II of Anjou, hoping to further tie his household to blood claims to the crown of England.

Philip Augustus was not merely a military strategist; he was also a shrewd student of administrative maneuvering. He curtailed the power of the wealthy counts, dukes, and lords that had bedeviled his predecessors, implementing various governmental reforms aimed at bolstering the central authority of the French monarchy.

Additionally, Philip II played a role in the urban development of French cities, with notable contributions to Paris, including the construction of the Louvre fortress and the expansion of city fortifications. Philip II's death in 1223 marked the end of a reign that laid the groundwork for the growth of royal power in France. His territorial acquisitions, diplomatic prowess, and administrative reforms primed France to become the preeminent power in Europe, changing the trajectory of the Capetian line from a family of nominal and powerless kings to a dynasty of formidable monarchs.

With Philip II dead, his son by Isabella of Hainault, Louis, became King Louis VIII. His reign was short-lived, lasting only from 1223 to 1226, but he spent the majority of his time on the throne establishing Capetian power in the southern portion of France. Though his father had concentrated on gathering the lands near Île-de-France, he had also loosely supported expansion into the southern half of the kingdom. Louis VIII is often remembered for adding the western province of Poitou on the border with Aquitaine into the real estate holdings of the Capet kings, but it is his attention to the southern territory of Languedoc that is emphasized more frequently.

A Christian sect known as Catharism had gained traction in the Languedoc area. The Cathars, often referred to as Albigensians thanks to their concentration around the town of Albi, adhered to a set of beliefs deemed heretical by the Catholic Church during the medieval period. Central to Cathar theology was a dualistic worldview, positing the existence of two cosmic principles—one associated with goodness and spirituality and the other with evil and the material world. This departure from traditional Christian monotheism, which recognizes a singular benevolent God, marked a fundamental difference in their beliefs.

A key aspect of Catharism was the repudiation of the material world as inherently corrupt and sinful. This rejection manifested in strict ascetic practices and a disdain for worldly pleasures. Additionally, Cathars rejected the sacraments of the Catholic Church, including baptism, communion, and marriage rites, considering them corrupted and spiritually insignificant. Cathars also held distinctive views on scripture, dismissing portions of the Bible, especially the Old Testament, which they associated with the creator of the material world. Certain teachings from the New Testament, including the Epistles, were also rejected. The movement had a hierarchical structure, distinguishing between their clergy, *perfecti*, who underwent special spiritual rituals, and the *credentes*, or "believers." However, the sect did embrace a general equality between the genders of male and female, in stark contrast to the attitudes of the time.

Nevertheless, the Cathar beliefs directly challenged the authority of the Catholic Church, which was an affront the pope could hardly let pass. In the early thirteenth century, Pope Innocent III initiated the Albigensian, or Cathar, Crusade in response to the perceived heretical threat of the Cathars. Under the leadership of northern French barons, soldiers descended on the Languedoc region, beginning with the siege of Béziers in 1209. When they finally gained access to the city, a horrifying command was supposedly uttered: *Caedite eos. Novit enim Dominus qui sunt eius.* This translates to "Kill them all, God will know His own," and resulted in the massacre of both Cathars and Catholics in the city.

The conflict continued, spanning several decades and culminating in the Treaty of Paris in 1229. This agreement brought the Languedoc region under the control of the French crown, marking the end of overt Cathar resistance and the beginning of the monarchy's control in the southern portion of France. Though Louis VIII had been deeply invested in the incorporation of Languedoc into his kingdom, he did not live to see his efforts come to fruition. He died, likely of dysentery, in 1226, three years before the ultimate conclusion of the Albigensian Crusade.

His young son, Louis IX, ascended to the throne at the tender age of twelve, though his mother, the fearsome Blanche of Castile, would act as his regent until 1234. Commonly known as Saint Louis, Louis IX is particularly celebrated for his unwavering commitment to religion and piety, though his reign was characterized by a dedication to growing the centralized monarchy initiated by his grandfather, aiming to diminish the power of feudal lords and fortify royal authority through administrative reforms.

Louis IX's patronage extended to the cultural sphere, where he supported the construction of Sainte-Chapelle in Paris[12], renowned for its exquisite Gothic architecture and stained-glass windows. His sponsorship of scholarly activities and manuscript production further contributed to cultural flourishing during his reign. It is his personal chaplain, Robert de Sorbon, who established the famed French university the Sorbonne in 1257. Known for his morality, Louis IX led a modest life, exemplifying Christian virtues through acts of charity and kindness. His commitment to morality shaped his conduct and influenced his approach to governance and foreign policy.

Unlike his father and grandfather before him, Louis IX chose to approach France's historic rivalry with the English with grace. After all, though family ties never really stopped the bloodshed in European history, the king of France and the king of England were now brothers-in-law. Louis IX married Margaret of Provence in 1234, and two years later, her sister Eleanor of Provence went on to wed Henry III Plantagenet. He was interested in solving the historic conflict between the two countries with diplomatic means, which was achieved in 1259 with the Treaty of Paris. This allowed Henry III of England to regain power over land in Guyenne—a portion of Aquitaine—in exchange for relinquishing further Plantagenet claims to Normandy, Anjou, Maine, Touraine, and Poitou. One year earlier, Louis had used this same diplomatic method to solve territorial disputes with his neighbors to the south via the Treaty of Corbeil. Louis surrendered French claims to Catalonia and Roussillon to acquire Barcelona's claims of Gévaudan and Rouergue.

Louis IX earned the moniker "Saint Louis" for his strong Christian faith and participation in two crusades in the Holy Land—the Seventh Crusade from 1248 to 1254 and the Eighth Crusade that claimed his life in 1270. He was later canonized as a saint by Pope Boniface VIII in 1297. Saint Louis is remembered as a symbol of stability, piety, and cultural advancement in medieval France.

The Capetian monarchy continued without too much drama into the 1300s. Louis IX's grandson, King Philip IV "The Fair," continued his great-great grandfather's work of consolidating the French Empire. His marriage to Joan I of Navarre brought the territories of Navarre and Champagne along with it. In a similar method, he wed his son to the heiress of the County of Burgundy in 1295 and went on to annex Lyon and southern Flanders in 1312. The French monarch was able to continually access greater and greater power thanks to his expansionary efforts, but he still desired stronger authority, particularly over ecclesiastical matters. The pope's ability to stand over all the temporal kings of Europe proved a long-term threat to the might of the French throne, but if the monarch had an increased say in who the pope was and what he could do, that would be a great boon.

In 1309, such a gift was presented to Philip IV when the newly elected Pope Clement V moved the papal residence from Rome in Italy to Avignon in the Provence region of France. Originally christened Bertrand de Got, Pope Clement V made the pivotal decision to relocate to Avignon for a confluence of political and strategic reasons. Elected as pope just four years earlier, Clement V's ascension was orchestrated with significant influence from the French monarchy, who sought a pope sympathetic to French interests.

The move to Avignon served as a strategic retreat from the intricate and often tumultuous political landscape of Italy, particularly in Rome, the historical seat of the papacy. Avignon, technically situated within the Papal States but still under the French crown's direct sway, offered a more stable and secure environment. Beyond its strategic advantages, Avignon's location in France was a key factor. This geographical closeness facilitated streamlined communication and coordination between the pope and the French monarchy, aligning with the broader objective of having a papacy more directly responsive to French concerns.

The relocation to Avignon marked the onset of the Avignon Papacy, also known as the Babylonian Captivity, a period during which multiple popes resided in Avignon. This move not only reshaped the dynamics of the papacy but also set the stage for challenges to its independence and legitimacy as it became increasingly intertwined with French politics.

The Avignon Papacy faced increasing criticism and challenges to papal legitimacy. The move weakened the papacy's moral authority and preceded a profound crisis: the Great, or Western Schism. In an attempt to restore papal authority and address concerns about the Avignon Papacy, Pope Gregory XI returned the papacy to Rome in 1376. However, his sudden death in 1378 became a catalyst for the schism. The College of Cardinals elected Pope Urban VI in Rome, but his confrontational style and disputes with the Cardinals led to dissatisfaction. In response, a faction of cardinals elected Pope Clement VII (now styled as Antipope Clement

VII by history) in Avignon in the same year, giving rise to a division in the Catholic Church. With two popes claiming legitimacy, the Great Schism unfolded, leading to a split in allegiances among the faithful. Ultimately, the Council of Constance was convened from 1414 to 1418 to address the schism. Pope Gregory XII of Rome and Antipope Benedict XIII of Avignon were persuaded to resign, and a new pope, Martin V, was elected to reunify the Church.

As the religious crisis roiled in Europe, further disruptions to medieval life occurred: the terrifying duo of famine and plague stalked the continent, unleashing a horrific loss of life. The Great Famine of the fourteenth century, often termed the Medieval Famine or the Great European Famine, saw widespread food shortages across Europe early in the century. In France, the calamity struck in multiple waves, but its most severe phase occurred between 1315 and 1317, affecting most of the European continent.

A convergence of factors contributed to the famine, but weather was largely to blame. A succession of cold, rainy summers and harsh winters disrupted agricultural activities, leading to extensive crop failures. The rain seemed near constant, flooding out low-lying areas and making fields boggy and unproductive. To add to the trouble, the predominant reliance on a single crop—grain, including wheat, oats, and barley—made the agricultural system particularly vulnerable. With less vegetation to sustain them, the people of medieval France had little else to fall back on since livestock, too, suffered due to the scarcity of fodder. For some, starvation became the only choice.

The economic repercussions were substantial. Crop failures led to skyrocketing food prices, plunging vast segments of the population into poverty and unemployment. Disruptions in trade and commerce were widespread as people grappled with the challenge of securing basic necessities. Socially, the famine fueled discontent and unrest. Economic hardships translated into a breakdown of social order, and rumors of widespread infanticide and cannibalism spread throughout Europe. It is estimated that around a tenth of Europe's population was slain by the Great Famine. Furthermore, there was a profound demographic impact beyond the immediate socio-economic consequences. Widespread malnutrition and weakened immune systems left populations vulnerable to all manner of maladies, setting the stage for the ruinous effects of the Black Death, which cast a long shadow over Europe in the mid-fourteenth century.

The Black Death, a devastating pandemic with origins in Central Asia, traces its roots to that continent's vast steppes where the bacterium *Yersinia pestis (Y. pestis)* thrived among the fleas living off rodent populations. While the bacterium had existed for thousands of years before the 1300s—scientists have found evidence of the disease in the remains of Neolithic humans—there was an explosion of the infection beginning in the early half of the fourteenth century.

Exactly how the disease arrived in Europe is still somewhat a mystery to scholars, though several hypotheses exist. The most popular and commonly repeated one is that trade routes and maritime transportation were responsible for introducing *Y. pestis* to the European continent. The Silk Road, connecting Asia to Europe, is considered a major transmission route. Merchants and travelers traversing these overland routes may have carried the bacterium-infested fleas on their goods, animals, or clothing. Another path considered is trade from the Black Sea region. Italian merchant ships transported infected rodents and fleas, and the arrival of these ships in Italian ports, like Messina in Sicily, is often associated with the initial outbreak in Europe.

Another incident often linked to the outset of the Black Death is the siege of Kaffa. In the early 1340s, the city of Kaffa (present-day Feodosiya, Ukraine) was a bustling Genoese trading hub strategically positioned on the Crimean Peninsula. The Mongol army, led by Jani Beg, laid siege to the city in 1345, hoping to win control of its lucrative trade routes. Amid the siege, the Black Death broke out among the combined Mongol-Tatar forces, devasting their ranks. Allegedly, the Mongols then resorted to biological warfare by throwing the bodies of their dead comrades over the city walls via catapult into Kaffa, with the intent of spreading the disease in the city. Naturally, this had the desired effect. Kaffa became infested with the plague, leading the Genoese to abandon the city by 1346.

The fleeing Genoese ships, carrying the refugees from Kaffa and the contagion, set sail for other Genoese-controlled territories. Some of these ships, laden with infected individuals, goods, and likely the rats carrying the fateful fleas, arrived at various Mediterranean ports, bringing the Black Death to Europe's doorstep.

Though the exact transmission route remains unclear, it was likely a combination of factors that included the movement of trade, the conflict at Kaffa, and the general migratory actions of humanity that brought the Black Death into

Europe. It happened at an awful time since the Great Famine had already decimated the health and immunity of a large swath of Europe's population. Whatever the initial cause, the Black Death began to spread in Europe in the 1340s and continued to echo through the continent for a decade. The convergence of ecological and environmental factors, combined with the movement of people along trade routes, created the perfect storm for the rapid and widespread dissemination of the plague across the continent.

Y. pestis is responsible for three types of plague: bubonic, pneumonic, and septicemic. The bubonic variety was the main culprit in the Black Death. However, the pneumonic plague, which spreads from person to person via aerosols like a cough or a sneeze, was likely also in play. It is a nasty illness typically transmitted through the bites of infected fleas often carried by rats, though it can also be contracted through direct contact with infected tissues or bodily fluids. The period of time from infection to the onset of symptoms usually lasts a few days, at which point a fever, chills, overall weakness, and muscle aches manifest. The main hallmark of the bubonic plague is the development of painful and swollen lymph nodes, known as buboes, in the groin, armpit, or neck. If left untreated, the bacteria multiplies and spreads through the bloodstream, resulting in a systemic infection that can bring a high fever, rapid heartbeat, and abdominal pain.

The bubonic plague can be treated with antibiotics, but in the 1300s, that was not an option. As a result, organ failure and death were common results of plague infection. The World Health Organization (WHO) currently sets the case-fatality rate for the bubonic plague at thirty to sixty percent, a figure largely contingent on prompt and proper treatment. The WHO also notes that the pneumonic plague, a more virulent form of the disease, can be almost universally fatal if left untreated. The exact death toll in Europe during the fourteenth century is unknown, but it is estimated to have taken thirty to fifty percent of the entire population of the continent. That is roughly twenty-five to forty million people.

In France, the disease spread rapidly across both urban centers and rural communities, with a twenty-five to fifty percent mortality rate. The trail of tragedy had profound consequences. Social disruption was severe, and communities grappled with sudden and widespread death. Families and neighborhoods struggled to cope with the immense loss of life, and the fabric of society was torn. Economically, the unexpected drop in the labor force led to labor shortages and rising wages, both of which posed a challenge to the necessity of a stable workforce for the established feudal system. This would be tested by unrest from the peasants, particularly in the Jacquerie in the 1350s, but this will be expounded upon later.

Culturally and psychologically, the pandemic imprinted trauma and existential angst onto the French populace. The Dance of Death[13], or *Danse Macabre*, became a recurring motif in medieval art, symbolizing the omnipresence and fragility of mortality. Even when the initial wave of the Black Plague subsided, resurgences and later waves continued to haunt France for the next two hundred or so years.

Beyond the immediate devastation, the Black Death brought about long-term demographic changes. The population decline and persistent labor shortages altered the power dynamics between the nobility and common people, contributing to the gradual erosion of the feudal system and ushering in a new chapter characterized by social, economic, and cultural transformations that would shape the country for generations to come.

As famine and death stalked France, there was yet another horseman on the loose: war. In 1328, Charles IV of France, the last of the Capet kings, passed away without a male heir. The question of who would succeed him to the French throne became a contentious issue that directly contributed to the outbreak of the Hundred Years' War between France and England.

The absence of a direct male from the Capet family line spawned two primary contenders: Edward II of England and Philip VI of France. Edward was Charles IV's nephew and the son of Isabella, his sister. Philip VI, on the other hand, was Charles IV's first cousin. The French nobility, adhering to the principle of Salic law—the ancient Frankish law code from the 500s CE—argued that the French crown could not pass through the female line. This caused the nobility to favor Philip VI's claim over Edward III's, and he was crowned in 1328 as the legitimate successor and closest direct male descendant. Thus, the monarchy moved from the Capet family to a cadet branch on the tree, the House of Valois.

At first, Philip VI's reign seemed promising; he regained control over Flanders and secured Edward III's acknowledgment of his sovereignty over the Duchy of Aquitaine. This alone would have nullified Edward III's claim to the French throne—but alas, the old rivals were not so easily pacified. By 1336, Philip VI appeared primed to support the Scottish King David II in his war against the English. At the same time, Philip VI declared Edward III to be in violation of feudal law and ordered Aquitaine to be seized. In a rage, Edward III renounced his previous fealty of Aquitaine to the French crown and reinstated his claim to all of France. This, plus the initial rejection of Edward III's claim, longstanding territorial disputes dating back to the holdings of the Plantagenets in the tenth and eleventh centuries, and various economic rivalries between the two nations, created a volatile situation that erupted into open conflict, marking the beginning of the Hundred Years' War in 1337.

In the early phases of the conflict, notably the battles of Sluys and Crécy, the English proved the effectiveness of their longbowmen against the French cavalry and crossbowmen. With the English carrying the day at both Sluys and Crécy, it seemed the French were no match for the English soldiers. Despite the French having a numerical advantage over their historic rivals, this did not matter in the face of England's technical edge. As a result, French casualties were quite high.

Amid the calamity, a peasant uprising broke out in 1358 in the northern Beauvais region. Known as the Jacquerie due to the French tendency to refer to peasants as "Jacques," this was a fervent uprising of rural peasants in the face of the oppressive feudal conditions they lived under. Emerging in the aftermath of the devastating Black Death, the revolt found its roots in the peasants' discontent with feudal obligations, exorbitant taxes, and economic exploitation imposed by the ruling nobility.

Commencing in May 1358, the uprising swiftly spread across northern France, fueled by a desire for improved conditions and a resistance to the oppressive measures imposed by the nobility. The revolt took a violent turn as peasants engaged in acts of retribution, pillaging castles and targeting nobles in a bid to address perceived injustices.

Facing the threat of the rebellion, the French nobility responded with force, mobilizing to suppress the uprising. The quelling of the Jacquerie involved brutal reprisals and marked a reinforcement of feudal structures, reasserting noble dominance over the peasant class. Although the immediate impact of the revolt did not result in a lasting transformation of the cultural order, it drew attention to the deep-seated social and economic grievances harbored by the peasantry.

France, knocked back on its heels by famine, plague, internal rebellion, and losses to the English, continued to fare poorly during the first phase of the Hundred Years' War. Two years before the Jacquerie, they had suffered a devastating defeat at the Battle of Poitiers at the hands of the English Prince Edward ("the Black Prince"). Both sides suffered heavy losses, but the French came out on the losing end, with their current king, John (Jean) II, captured by the English and the French army left in ruins.

Languishing in captivity for several years, John II finally inked a treaty with Edward III on May 8, 1360. The Treaty of Brétigny (Brittany) sought to introduce a temporary cessation of hostilities and outline terms for a semblance of peace. The treaty delineated substantial territorial concessions to England, including Aquitaine, Gascony, Calais, Ponthieu,

124 | DOMINIC HAYNES

and others, greatly shrinking the holdings that John II's Capetian ancestors had worked so hard to amass. Secondly, the treaty stipulated a substantial ransom for John II's release. France could not afford to pay the monetary sum, so prisoners were accepted in John II's stead, one of them being his second son, Prince Louis. Prince Louis escaped, and John II returned to England on his own accord, living the remaining four years of his life in London.

With England receiving land and prisoners, the main gain for France was Edward III's formal renunciation of his claim to the French crown. This acknowledged the autonomy of the French monarchy and simultaneously consolidated strictly English control over his extensive new territories. With both countries ravaged by famine and disease, a period of relative calm was welcomed on all sides, and the agreements founded in the Treaty of Brétigny were finalized in the Treaty of Calais in October of the same year. A truce was finally established, providing a temporary respite from the relentless hostilities. However, the underlying tensions and territorial disputes remained, eventually leading to the resumption of conflict in subsequent phases of the Hundred Years' War.

Life remained difficult in France. The ravages of the war and the pandemic were incalculable, and now soldiers, underpaid and starving, were roaming the countryside and taking what they could from those with lesser means. With King John II gone, his son, Charles V, followed him onto the throne in 1364. At first, he honored the Treaties of Brétigny and Calais, but he did maintain that he was owed authority in Aquitaine. Aside from the English, Charles V also found himself beset by squabbles among the nobles, and he became occupied with securing the loyalty of various kingdoms and duchies.

Times were also tough in England, and the Black Prince Edward, who had been given Aquitaine by his father, Edward III of England, levied harsh taxes in the region in hopes of securing more funds. Before long, the old tensions between England and France resurfaced, and nine years after the treaties of Brétigny and Calais, war broke out once more. This time, however, the French were better prepared.

Firstly, a French alliance with the Kingdom of Castile nullified England's naval supremacy. Secondly, Charles V abandoned the previous strategies of large pitched battles against the renowned English infantry and longbowmen, opting instead for guerrilla warfare and scorched earth tactics. This approach aimed to disrupt English supply lines and wear down their forces through attrition rather than direct confrontation. He managed to retake the western provinces of Guyenne and Poitou, though strategic port towns like Calais and Bordeaux remained in English custody.

This momentum did not continue indefinitely. In 1375, the Truce of Bruges marked a temporary pause in hostilities, but it was fleeting. The following year, the Franco-Papal alliance that had been established at the beginning of the century under King Philip IV at long last collapsed when Pope Gregory XI returned to Rome in 1376, ending the Avignon Papacy. Charles supported Robert of Geneva in the next papal election, but it was Pope Urban VI who ended up taking the papal crown in Rome. Ultimately, Robert of Geneva was elected as Antipope Clement VII at the outset of the Great Schism, but this was no political help to the French crown.

In 1377, Edward III of England died, leaving an unstable and war-weary kingdom to his grandson, Richard II. Three short years later, Charles V followed his old nemesis to the grave. His son, Charles VI, took the throne without any issues, but the Hundred Years' War raged onward even with new kings.

Not long after his accession, Charles VI faced a fierce rebellion from the Flemish towns in the north led by Ghent. This was ultimately quashed at the Battle of Roosebeke in 1382, and the leader of the Flemish rebellion was executed. Another attempt at peace was brokered between Charles VI and Richard II with the Truce of Leulinghem in 1389. This set forth a twenty-seven-year armistice between the nations to give them time to deal with other internal and external threats.

Nevertheless, hostilities, particularly over the territory of Aquitaine, remained potent. In 1399, a new king in England, Henry IV, renewed the old English claim to the French throne, and the struggle began once more. The royal families of Europe were all linked through various marriages, which made the question of succession rather thorny at times. Henry IV was the maternal grandson of the current king of France, and though claims to the throne via female lines had proved fruitless in the past, it was upon this blood tie that he based his right to the French crown.

However, it would be his son, Henry V, who would truly turn the tide in favor of the English once more. The famous Battle of Agincourt in October 1415 was the culmination of his campaigns in northern France, resulting in a significant victory for England. Despite being heavily outnumbered, the English longbowmen and men-at-arms were victorious over the larger French forces, suffering relatively low casualties in contrast to the heavy toll exacted from their enemies.

In the aftermath of Agincourt, diplomatic negotiations between England and France intensified. The Treaty of Troyes in 1420 stipulated that Henry V would marry Princess Catherine, daughter of Charles VI of France, and thus be recognized as the legitimate heir to the French throne, effectively bypassing Charles VI's son, the Dauphin Charles, and uniting the English and French crowns. Henry V now had control over large portions of northern France, but the long-term success of this was affected by his death only two years after the signing of the Treaty of Troyes.

The same year that Henry V died, so too did Charles VI. With this, the succession of the French throne was once again a central point of conflict. The Treaty of Troyes stipulated that Henry V's son, Henry VI, should be the new king. However, Charles VI had a son, Charles VII, who most French people believed to be their rightful king. One such person was Joan of Arc (Jeanne d'Arc), a peasant girl from a small village in the northeastern portion of France. From a young age, she allegedly experienced visions and voices that urged her to support the dauphin, Charles VII, when the time came.

One of Joan's earliest successes came in 1429 during the Siege of Orléans. Despite initial skepticism from military leaders, Joan managed to convince Charles VII to allow her to accompany the French army. Her presence and leadership supposedly inspired the troops, and the siege was lifted in

May of the same year. This victory boosted French morale after years of defeat at the hands of the English.

From Orléans, Joan accompanied Charles VII to Rheims, where he was crowned on July 17, solidifying his legitimacy as the rightful king of France. Sadly, she was captured by Burgundians and handed over to the English in 1431, facing charges of heresy and witchcraft. She was deemed guilty and burned at the stake in Rouen on May 30, 1431.

Despite the setback of losing Joan, Charles VII seemed to be finally putting out the fires of instability around his kingdom. In 1435, he signed the Treaty of Arras with the Duchy of Burgundy, establishing peace to his east. He and Henry VI signed the Treaty of Tours just under ten years later. This renewable agreement essentially maintained the current status of the French borders, with England retaining ownership over Maine, Bordelais, Calais, and most of Normandy. This was further bolstered by the wedding of the English king to Margaret of Anjou, a niece of the French king's wife.

Despite increased diplomacy, Charles VII was still interested in bringing territory back under his crown. After first securing a diplomatic agreement from Henry VI to surrender Maine, he followed that up with the threat of military violence when the English king was slow to honor his promises. Before long, Charles VII abandoned his diplomatic pretenses and began seizing English-held portions of France, working to slowly recapture NOrmandy. After the Battle of Formigny in 1450, Normandy was once more under French control.

The final engagement of the Hundred Years' War was the Battle of Castillon in 1453. French forces led by Jean Bureau decisively defeated the English in Gascony, marking the end of English attempts to regain control over French territories. The prolonged war, coupled with the other economic and social strains on both kingdoms, had taken quite a toll, and England and France were eager for peace. At this point, the English had lost the majority of their territorial gains on the continent, and only Calais, a port city on the western edge of France, remained under English control.

Despite the general cessation of conflict, intermittent skirmishes continued, forcing King Louis XI of France and Edward IV of England to the table in 1475 to work out a final resolution to the prolonged war. The Treaty of Picquigny gave financial compensation to the English in exchange for the final withdrawal of their claims to French territory. In the end, the English crown was able to maintain control over Calais until its capture just under a century later. The end of the war marked a turning point for France, allowing the nation to consolidate its territories and strengthen its central authority.

With the strife of the last century laid aside at long last, France could focus on growth and stability as the Renaissance dawned.

7

RENAISSANCE AND RELIGION
(1475–1610 CE)

With the endless trudge of the Hundred Years' War set aside, one would hope there would be a relative period of peace. However, though there were no conflicts on the same level as the previous century, the next hundred years still proved to be full of friction and discord. Still, though life was not easy, it was at least less terrifying than the fourteenth century. Despite continual political squabbles, royal infighting, and scrabbling for European supremacy, the cultural backdrop of the Renaissance provided a fertile ground for intellectual and artistic growth in France.

In 1461, Louis XI became the king of France. Known as "Louis the Prudent" or "Louis the Spider," his reign was characterized by astute political maneuvering, a fervent drive to centralize power, and a relentless pursuit of royal authority. From an early age, he was aware that he was not conventionally attractive, which likely honed other traits that served him well throughout his tenure as king. Intelligent and cunning, he inspired loyalty in his soldiers and subjects, while his constant bureaucratic machinations kept many nobles on their toes. At the beginning of his rule, he was still grappling with the vestiges of the Hundred Years' War. As mentioned in the previous chapter, it was under his monarchy that the Treaty of Picquigny was signed in 1475, re-establishing French supremacy over England on the European continent.

Early in his reign, Louis XI was interested in continuing the work of his predecessors in cementing the centrality of the monarchy in French life. These early stirrings toward absolutism influenced the trajectory of his successors and likely set France on the political path it would take during the seventeenth and eighteenth centuries. However, there were challenges to his rule that impacted him from the beginning. The War of the Public Weal broke out in 1465, just four years after his rise to power. Fueled by discontent among the French nobility and regional leaders, the war emerged as a manifestation of grievances against Louis XI's centralizing policies.

Opposition to the monarchy stemmed from a coalition known as the League of the Public Weal, which was comprised of discontented nobles, including Louis XI's own brother Charles, Duke of Berry, and influential figures like the Duke of Brittany and the Duke of Burgundy, Charles the Bold. The league's primary objectives were to safeguard feudal privileges, limit royal authority, and address concerns over taxation and governance.

After a series of military engagements and some savvy political maneuvering, Louis XI utilized his strengths as a negotiator to dismantle the league, piece by piece, using a combination of promises, alliances, and some strategic but inconsequential concessions. The dissolution of the League of the Public Weal solidified Louis XI's position as a strong king. It allowed him to proceed with the centralization policies he wished to implement, neatly consolidating royal authority in his hands.

Louis XI embarked on a mission to curtail the influence of regional nobility, opting for a more consolidated governance structure. This involved expanding the role of royal officers in administering justice, collecting taxes, and enforcing royal policies. Concurrently, he forged alliances with the growing urban bourgeoisie, granting them privileges to foster economic growth and fortify the monarchy economically.

An obstacle to Louis XI's attempts to concentrate the crown's power was his old nemesis from the War of the Public Weal, Charles the Bold, the Duke of Burgundy. Burgundy, a duchy located in eastern France, had long been a thorn in the side of the French monarchy that Louis XI hoped to extract. The Burgundians were allied with the English, a relationship Louis XI wanted to sunder to weaken Burgundy. Though his initial attempts at foundering the Anglo-Burgundian alliance failed, Louis XI could indirectly debilitate the duchy by financing the Swiss Confederacy and the Duchy of Lorraine when the two entities went to war with Burgundy.

This investment proved fruitful in 1477 when Charles the Bold was slain at the Battle of Nancy. With only a daughter, Mary of Burgundy, left surviving to inherit Charles' lands, Louis XI pounced on the duchy, eager to parcel it up and claim ownership on behalf of the French crown. However, his enthusiasm was checked by Mary's husband, Archduke Maximilian (later Holy Roman Emperor Maximilian I), who was prepared to defend his wife's inheritance. Though not as climactic as seizing his rival's territory before he was cold in his grave, with the Treaty of Arras in 1482, Louis XI eventually got most of what he wanted.

Though Burgundian lands did not pass into his possession legally, he was recognized as the sovereign of the Duchy of Burgundy as well as the regions of Picardy and Boulonnais. Furthermore, Maximilian and Mary's daughter, Margaret of Austria, was promised as a bride to Louis XI's son and heir, Charles, bringing the region of Franche-Comté with her as a dowry. Ultimately, this union would not come to fruition, as more pressing political matters pushed Charles VIII into matrimony with Anne of Brittany, leaving Margaret brokenhearted.

In another smooth political move, Louis XI secured a large tract of land for the crown by negotiating with René, Duke of Anjou, for his land. When René died in 1480, the crown re-absorbed Anjou for the final time. To recapitulate, during Louis XI's tenure, he brought Burgandy, Boulonnais, and Picardy under his authority and added the regions of Franche-Comté, Artois, Anjou, Maine, and Provence to the royal real estate portfolio. Louis XI essentially did away with the hegemony of the regional feudal powerbrokers, ushering in a new era where the crown truly stood above all.

As mentioned earlier, though Charles VIII had been promised to Margaret of Austria when King Louis XI died in 1483, eight years later, in 1491, Charles VIII wed Anne of Brittany. Lured by Anne's inheritance of the sizeable duchy of Brittany, Charles VIII was prepared to forfeit his previous fiancée's dowry of Franche-Comté to grasp the coveted territory.

However, the prize of Brittany wasn't Charles VIII's only goal. He was further enticed by the promise of land in Italy. In 1494, France invaded the peninsula, kicking off another lengthy period of war that did not conclude until the latter half of the 1500s. Due to a distant familial claim, Charles VIII's main target was the Kingdom of Naples in the southern portion of Italy. Simply put, Charles VIII's grandfather, Charles VII, had wed Marie of Anjou, a member of the ruling family of Naples, until 1442 when the House of Trastámara took the Neapolitan throne. Charles VIII saw Naples as his birthright due to this claim through his grandmother.

In 1494, Charles VIII crossed the Alps with his army, entering Italy to pursue his territorial ambitions. His forces encountered minimal resistance initially, as many Italian states were unprepared for the scale of the French invasion. This allowed his company to move swiftly down the Italian peninsula. By 1495, Naples fell to the French, and Charles VIII was crowned the King of Naples.

The rapid success of Charles VIII's campaign alarmed other Italian states and various European powers, including the Papal States, Spain, and the Holy Roman Empire. With increasing resistance and diplomatic pressures, Charles VIII agreed to the Treaty of Granada in 1495. The treaty stipulated his withdrawal from Italy in exchange for various concessions, marking the end of his personal ambitions in

Italy, though the French desire for Naples would continue under his successor, Louis XII.

While Charles VIII was preparing for another foray into Italy, he passed away in 1498. The French king had no living children and no clear successors to follow him. His children with Anne of Brittany had not lived to see adulthood, sparking another succession crisis. The closest male relative was a distant cousin, Louis, Duke of Orléans, a member of the Orléans branch of the Valois family, and the great-grandson of King Charles V (r. 1364–1380). Initially wed to his cousin Joan (Jeanne) in a bid by King Louis XI to end the Orléans line—she was disabled and considered sterile—this marriage was annulled by Pope Alexander VI in 1498 in preparation for his ascension to the throne.

To restore his legitimacy and keep Brittany tied to the French crown, the newly minted Louis XII married Charles VIII's widow, Anne of Brittany. For the most part, Louis XII pursued the same goals as his predecessor, returning to campaign once more in Italy. At first, he managed some military successes, taking Milan and Naples, but he had difficulty holding them. Milan was retaken by the Sforza family after a matter of months in 1499, while Naples was lost by the French in 1504 thanks to the efforts of King Ferdinand II of Aragon.

However, skirmishing along the Italian peninsula continued for most of his reign, with many of the monarchs of the day joining in, including Holy Roman Emperor Maximilian I and King Henry VIII of England. Most of the European monarchs, along with the current pope, ended up allying against Louis XII, isolating him on the continent and forcing him to check his expansionary ambitions. Signing the Anglo-French Peace of London in August of 1514 with Henry VIII, a freshly widowed Louis XII was able to tamp down the hostilities between the two nations. His marriage to Henry VIII's sister, Mary Tudor, furthered this in October of the same year.

Despite his diplomatic and military failures, Louis XII was well-loved at home and referred to as the "Father of the People." This was thanks to his policies that protected the lower classes and less fortunate from oppression and undue financial burdens. He also managed to finance most of his military conflicts without raising taxes, keeping him popular among the rich and poor.

When he died at age fifty-two in 1515, his mixed legacy kept him in a favorable place in his subjects' hearts despite his political missteps and ineptitudes. With only one illegitimate son and two legitimate daughters, the question of succession loomed large once more. However, unlike his predecessor, Louis did have an heir in mind. Francis, the son of the Count of Angoulême, was a cousin of the late king and a member of the Angoulême branch of the Valois royal family. In 1498, he was named the heir apparent and gained the Duchy of Valois. However, Louis XII did not trust his young cousin. He chose to keep him out on the military frontline rather than educate him on matters of the state. This would come back to haunt him, for though he was well-educated, intelligent, and curious, his inexperience made him overly trusting and a generally poor politician. Before Louis XII died, he wed his daughter, Claude of France, to Francis, ensuring both his legacy and a smooth transfer of power for the young king.

Francis I, ultimately quite a prominent French monarch, ended up reigning from 1515 to 1547 and became a key figure during the Renaissance. He was a patron of the arts and created a courtly environment that encouraged intellectual and artistic exploration and growth. Inviting high-caliber artists like Leonardo da Vinci to his court, he fostered a deep cultural exchange with other European nations, particularly with the cradle of the Renaissance: Italy. Thanks to his interest and passion for all things intellectual and artistic, France became a flourishing hub of creativity and learning.

In greater detail, the Renaissance in France spanned roughly from the late fifteenth to the early sixteenth century. It marked a period of cultural, artistic, and intellectual revival. While the Italian Renaissance is better remembered, the French Renaissance had unique characteristics and contributions to art, architecture, literature, and education.

Artists such as Jean Clouet and his son François excelled in detailed and delicate portraiture. Jean was one of Francis I's chief painters and captured the king's likeness[14] as well as that of other well-known nobles. He was also known for his religious work, such as his paintings titled *Saint Jerome* and *Four Evangelists*. His son, François, continued in his father's footsteps, remaining at court as a painter for Francis I and his successors Henry (Henri) II, Francis II, and Charles IX. He sometimes published his artwork under his father's byname, making it difficult at times to know which Clouet created which works.

Aside from the royal painters, the School of Fontainebleau was also established under Francis I. Refurbishing an old medieval castle for the artists' use, Francis I convinced several Italian masters, including Rosso Fiorentino and Francesco Primaticcio, to relocate to France to work. Engravings, sculpture, and paintings were all common at Fontainebleau, and a style of artwork known as Mannerism —involving the depiction of dramatically elongated limbs and necks—became popular. Primaticcio, in particular, enjoyed utilizing Mannerism, and his works often featured scenes from Classical Greek mythology[15] or the life of Alexander the Great.

Although Italian styles remained exceedingly popular in architecture, French architects utilized Italian influence and blended it with their French sensibilities to create a unique style. The Château de Chambord[16] and the Château de Fontainebleau[17] are both fine examples of this blend of French and Italian Renaissance styles, featuring ornamental window frames and exterior moldings with multiple turrets, towers, and chimneys spiraling toward the sky.

As for intellectual endeavors, the advent of the printing press facilitated easier dissemination of ideas and knowledge, which contributed to the rampant spread of Renaissance thought throughout France. Humanism is one of the chief Renaissance movements, emphasizing the study of classical literature and philosophy. Two prominent humanist French scholars were Jacques Lefèvre d'Étaples and Guillaume Budé. Francis I, also considered a humanist, further pushed the growth of intellectualism in his kingdom by providing a center for humanist studies. The establishment of the Collège de France in 1530 emphasized his dedication to education during the Renaissance.

French humanists, along with philosophical leanings and educational aspirations, also produced great literature and poetry. François Rabelais, sometimes dubbed the "first great French prose author," was famous for his satirical work, particularly his pentology of novels, *Gargantua and Pantagruel*. Poetry also experienced a revival, with poets like Clément Marot contributing to the development of French literature with works like *L'Enfer* (The Inferno).

Francis I also took advantage of the scientific advancements that made the Age of Exploration possible, sending explorers on far-flung voyages across the Atlantic. In 1534, Jacques Cartier navigated Newfoundland and the St. Lawrence River on the North American continent. French influence in this New World grew, with the high point coming in the seventeenth century. At that time, France possessed holdings in the Caribbean, like the island of Martinique, much of what is today eastern Canada and the United States, as well as some smaller holdings in South America. Though they would later cede much of this territory to other European powers, their influence was still keenly felt throughout the New World.

Aside from his cultural and intellectual pursuits, Francis I continued the Italian Wars that had haunted his two predecessors. Like Charles VIII, he was very interested in expanding French influence in Italy, and this brought him into direct conflict with the large and powerful Habsburg family, who controlled much of the region. He won a victory early in his reign at the Battle of Marignano in 1515, establishing his reputation as a competent military leader, though he failed to garner any lasting hold on the Italian peninsula.

Though Francis I cultivated a rivalry with Henry VIII of England, it was not as acrimonious as his dislike of the Holy Roman Emperor Charles V. This drove him to seek a relationship with the English king that waffled between friendship and enmity for the duration of both kings' reigns. After all, Francis I had promised his son, the Dauphin, to Henry VIII's young daughter, Mary. However, this engagement fell through after a few years, much like the rest of the pair's diplomatic endeavors.

In 1520, Francis I met with Henry VIII of England in a grand diplomatic and cultural event near Calais known as the Field of the Cloth of Gold. The meeting aimed to strengthen relations between the two kingdoms, but it also showcased the opulence and splendor of the French court in a bid to impress his English counterpart. During the festivities, the English and French monarchs pledged lasting peace between their two kingdoms.

Francis I's luck ran out in 1525. Interested in re-taking Milan, Francis I launched a campaign into Lombardy and laid siege to the city of Pavia. This proved unsuccessful since the town was well-fortified, causing the French troops to withdraw. On their way out, Francis I and his forces encountered the joint Imperial-Spanish army led by Charles V and engaged in open conflict. The battle proved disastrous for the French. Despite initial successes, a combination of factors, including rugged terrain and unexpected attacks, led to the collapse of the French position. Francis I himself was captured during the chaos of the battle.

His captivity in Madrid lasted over a year until the signing of the Treaty of Madrid in 1526, in which he agreed to give up certain territories in exchange for his release. In short, Francis I was forced to renounce all his claims to Italy, Artois, and Flanders, and he handed Burgundy over to Charles V. Furthermore, two of his sons were sent to the Spanish court to remain hostages. However, Francis I later repudiated the treaty, claiming it was made under duress. He allied once more with Henry VIII against the Habsburgs, but after Charles V sacked Rome in 1527, Francis I was forced to give up his Italian dreams once and for all through the Treaty of Cambrai in 1529. Francis I's later years were marred by continued conflicts with Charles V, the Habsburgs, and Henry VIII. He died on March 31, 1547, and was succeeded by his son, Henry II.

Henry II continued much of his father's legacy, and his court remained an artistic and intellectual haven. This was further bolstered by his nuptials with the famed daughter of Florence, Catherine de' Medici, who brought an increased Italian influence to the courts of her husband and sons. Catherine is also responsible for the introduction of ballet— an art form that would become highly consequential to the French monarchy in the following century.

Conflicts with Charles V in Italy continued, but the Italian Wars finally ended in 1559. The Treaty of Cateau-Cambrésis marked the end of the fighting and brought about a peace settlement between France and the Habsburgs, who at the time held the reins of power in both Spain and the Holy Roman Empire. It solidified the Habsburgs' control over the Italian peninsula, establishing them as the preeminent European power for a time.

However, what Henry II and his sons and successors truly had to grapple with was the rising religious tension in France. The Reformation had kicked off shortly after the Renaissance, leading many to question the teachings of the Catholic Church. This religious and cultural movement that profoundly reshaped Europe was sparked by dissatisfaction with perceived corruption, doctrinal disputes, and abuses within the Catholic Church.

One of the key figures of the Reformation was Martin Luther, a German monk, who in 1517 famously nailed his *Ninety-Five Theses* to the door of the Wittenberg Castle Church(Schlosskirche), criticizing the sale of indulgences and questioning certain practices of the Church. Luther's ideas spread rapidly, and his translation of the Bible into German allowed more people to access the scriptures directly.

The movement gained momentum with the contributions of other reformers, such as the French exile John Calvin in Geneva and Ulrich Zwingli in Zurich. These leaders emphasized the authority of the Bible, salvation by faith alone, and the priesthood of all believers. The founding of Lutheranism under Martin Luther, Anglicanism under King Henry VIII, and Calvinism under John Calvin are all examples of breakaway sects from the Catholic Church that caused unrest throughout the European continent for the next several centuries.

The Reformation also had profound political consequences, contributing to conflicts such as the Wars of Religion in France and the Thirty Years' War in the Holy Roman Empire. Additionally, it fueled cultural and intellectual transformations, promoting literacy, individual interpretation of religious texts, and new forms of worship. Violence, war, questions of succession, and more were all justified through a religious lens by Protestants and Catholics alike.

The Council of Trent, convened by the Catholic Church in response to the Reformation, initiated the Counter-Reformation, a series of reforms within the Catholic Church aimed at addressing some of the concerns raised by the Protestants. Despite the religious divisions it caused, the Reformation ultimately played a crucial role in shaping the modern religious and political landscape of Europe.

France experienced significant religious tension between Protestants, known in that part of Europe as Huguenots, and Catholics, marking a period known as the French Wars of Religion. As the Protestant Reformation reached France, Calvinism, in particular, gained traction among both the nobility and urban elites, creating a minority Huguenot population in a predominantly Catholic country. Political and religious affiliations became intertwined, with the French monarchy predominantly Catholic and some influential noble families converting to Calvinism. One such family was the Bourbons, a cadet branch of the Capetian Family that ruled Navarre and later, France.

The French Wars of Religion spanned from 1562 to 1598 and spawned a series of conflicts and civil wars between Catholic and Huguenot factions. Though tensions were already high between the two groups, the inception of out-and-out hostilities can be traced to the Massacre of Vassy (in French, the *Massacre de Wassy*) in 1562. Located in north-eastern France, Vassy became the site of a violent clash between Catholic forces and Protestant Huguenots. The conflict erupted during a worship service attended by predominantly Huguenot followers.

Francis, Duke of Guise, a prominent Catholic leader and a member of the highly influential Guise family, led an armed force to disrupt this Protestant assembly, viewing it as a challenge to the authority of the Catholic Church. The confrontation quickly escalated into a brutal massacre, resulting in the deaths of numerous Huguenots and injuring many more. The Massacre of Vassy intensified preexisting religious tensions and marked the beginning of the French Wars of Religion.

The following year, in 1563, King Charles IX—likely under the influence of Catherine de' Medici, issued the Edict of Amboise in an attempt to bring a temporary resolution to the early conflicts of the French Wars of Religion. This edict aimed to address the grievances of the Huguenots and granted limited religious freedoms to Protestants, allowing them to worship in certain locations outside towns. Additionally, Huguenots were given the right to hold their religious services in one town per administrative district.

While the Edict of Amboise sought to ease tensions by providing a degree of religious tolerance, it fell short of establishing a lasting peace. The subsequent years witnessed a recurrence of hostilities, leading to further conflicts in the French Wars of Religion. The edict, however, marked an early attempt to find a compromise between the Catholic majority and the Protestant minority in a time of religious upheaval and foreshadowed later agreements between the two parties.

Catherine de' Medici, serving as regent for her sons, sought to navigate the complex religious landscape. However, her policies, aimed at maintaining a delicate balance, often led to temporary peace without addressing the underlying issues. The marriage of the Bourbon Henry of Navarre, a prominent Huguenot, to Catherine de' Medici's daughter, the Catholic Princess Margaret of Valois, in 1572, triggered the infamous St. Bartholomew's Day Massacre, resulting in widespread violence and thousands of Huguenot deaths.

The union of Henry and Margaret was intended to reconcile the two religious factions, and many prominent Huguenot leaders came to Paris to celebrate the wedding on August 18, 1572. However, on the night of August 22, an assassination attempt was made on the life of the Huguenot leader Gaspard de Coligny at Catherine de' Medici's instigation. Coligny survived, and the king promised a thorough investigation into the incident. Catherine, to cover her tracks, told her son that the Huguenots were planning a retaliatory attack for the attempt on Coligny's life. Perturbed by his mother's manipulations and failing to see them for what they were, Charles IX ordered a coordinated and violent attack on the Huguenots. In the bloodshed, Coligny was killed around dawn on the 24th by agents of the Catholic Guise family.

The brutality quickly escalated into a massacre in Paris and then spread to other parts of France, and the savagery continued for several days. Estimates of the number of casualties vary, but it is believed that thousands of Huguenots lost their lives. The St. Bartholomew's Day Massacre had a profound impact on the French Wars of Religion, intensifying already fraught religious tensions and leading to a resumption of hostilities between Catholics and Protestants.

After the notorious St. Bartholomew's Day Massacre intensified violence against Huguenots, subsequent conflicts continued, leading to the War of the Three Henrys from 1587 to 1589. This further complicated matters as Henry of Navarre, Henry III of France, and Henry of Guise vied for control.

Henry III, the reigning king at the time and the third son of Catherine de' Medici to take the French throne, was facing pressure from both Catholic and Protestant factions. On one side was the Catholic, or Holy, League, led by Henry, Duke of Guise, the oldest son and successor of Francis, the orchestrator of the Massacre of Vassy. They sought to establish a staunchly Catholic monarchy that resisted the influence of Protestantism.

On the other side stood Henry of Navarre, the son of Antoine de Bourbon, Duke of Vendôme, and Jeanne d'Albret, Queen of Navarre. Though he was known to be a direct and legitimate successor to the Capetian kings of France, the many sons born by Catherine de 'Medici made the reality of his French kingship seem unlikely. Raised as a Calvinist by his mother, he took the throne of Navarre upon her death in 1572, a small kingdom comprised of a portion of southern France and northern Spain. A Calvinist and the legitimate heir to the throne from the Protestant perspective, Henry of Navarre aimed to secure his rightful position as the heir to the throne when Catherine de' Medici's youngest son and heir presumptive, François, Duke of Anjou, died in 1584, leaving King Henry III of France with no clear successor.

This notion of a Protestant heir was intensely antagonistic to Henry of Guise, the Catholic League, and the pope. In the summer of 1585, Catherine de' Medici, acting on behalf of the French crown, signed a treaty with the Guise family to keep the peace between the powerful Catholic coalition and the French monarch. The Treaty of Nemours essentially forced the French crown to declare war on the Huguenots living within France's borders, barring them from holding political offices and severely curtailing their religious freedom. This edict was reinforced in the fall of the same year when Pope Sixtus V excommunicated Henry of Navarre and declared him unable to become the next king of France.

Fighting occurred mainly in southwestern France, and Henry of Navarre demonstrated his prowess and leadership skills. Initially, the French crown, under Henry III, aligned with the Guise family and the Catholic League to combat Protestant forces. However, the situation changed dramatically when the Catholic League attempted to install a Spanish princess (Philip II of Spain's daughter) as the monarch of France. Realizing that the Catholic League's ambitions threatened his own power, Henry III decisively turned against them. In 1588, he ordered the assassination of the Catholic League's influential leader, Henry, Duke of Guise. Following this, Henry III declared Henry of Navarre, a Protestant, as his successor. This decision, however, led to Henry III's own demise. In 1589, a radical member of the Catholic League, Jacques Clément, assassinated Henry III.

The war concluded with the Protestant Henry of Navarre emerging victorious, though he eventually converted to Catholicism to secure broader acceptance, supposedly stating, "Paris is well worth a mass." His accession as Henry IV marked the end of the Wars of Religion, and his reign saw efforts to reconcile the Catholic and Protestant factions through the Edict of Nantes in 1598, granting religious tolerance to the Huguenots and allowing them to worship freely and once again hold political office.

Known as Henry IV "the Great" or "the Good King," he returned unity, growth, and progress to a kingdom long devastated by internal strife. As the first Bourbon king, his policies aimed at fostering economic growth and reducing the impact of taxation on the peasantry. He cleared the national debt and created a reserve of eighteen million livres (a unit of account established by Charlemagne). Additionally, he initiated infrastructure projects, including the renovation of Paris, and oversaw the completion of the construction of the Pont Neuf, the oldest standing bridge across the Seine in Paris. He also completed the construction of the Tuileries, which was begun under Catherine de' Medici, built the great gallery of the Louvre, the north wing of the Hôtel-de-Ville, and the Place Royale (Place des Vosges), the oldest planned square in the city of Paris.

When it came to a successor, Henry IV was—at first—unlucky. Though it had spawned all the drama of the Saint Bartholomew's Day Massacre, his first marriage to Margaret of Valois failed in fruitfulness. The union was annulled by Pope Clement VIII, and Henry IV remarried Marie de' Medici, a relative of the late Queen Mother, Catherine. The two had more luck, with Marie bearing five children, one of whom was the dauphin, the future King Louis XIII.

Despite his glowing reputation in history's eyes, Henry IV faced opposition, and his reign ended tragically with his assassination by François Ravaillac, another religious fanatic like his predecessor's murderer, in 1610. Henry IV's reign is often remembered as a time of reconciliation and reconstruction following the religious strife of previous decades, setting the stage for the consolidation of royal power in the hands of the powerful Bourbon dynasty.

8

"L'ÉTAT, C'EST MOI": THE AGE OF ABSOLUTISM (1610–1794 CE)

The development of the centralized monarchy of France had been underway for some time, as far back as the days of the early Capetian kings like Philip Augustus (Philip II). Now, with the son of Henry of Navarre on the throne, the Bourbon line was poised to realize this centuries-long dream of their ancestors. Louis XIII of France, who reigned from 1610 to 1643, succeeded his father, Henry IV, at the age of nine. Given his youth, his mother and yet another Medici, Marie, served as regent until Louis XIII reached maturity. The early years of Louis XIII's reign were marked by the continuation of the policies initiated by his father, particularly those aimed at consolidating royal power and maintaining peace within the kingdom.

However, France was fragile, and religious differences still threatened the integrity of the kingdom, potentially unraveling all of Henry IV's work. Cardinal Richelieu was one of the key figures who rose during Louis XIII's early reign to address this crisis. Born Armand Jean du Plessis, Duke of

Richelieu, he served as Chief Minister to King Louis XIII from 1624 until he died in 1642. Initially beginning his career as a bishop, Richelieu's ascent to prominence occurred when he entered the service of the Queen Mother, Marie de' Medici, during her rule as Louis XIII's regent.

Several defining features characterized his tenure as chief minister. Richelieu aimed to bolster royal authority mainly by centralizing power within the monarchy. This involved curtailing the autonomy of regional nobility and diminishing their military influence, no matter the degree of prominence or power. Even members of the Bourbon family were not immune to Richelieu's reduction of noble power. Though he had begun his career working for Marie de' Medici, the two eventually fell out, with Marie and one of her other sons, Gaston, Duke of Orléans, initiating opposition to the powerful clergyman.

The souring of the relationship between Richelieu and Marie de' Medici came to a head on November 10, 1630. Known as the "Day of Dupes," this was a political crisis brought about by the power struggle between Marie and Richelieu. Essentially, Marie wanted to weaken Richelieu's hold on power and influence over her son, the king. Hoping to replace her rival with a weaker, more compliant minister, Marie pushed for Richelieu's expulsion. Sensing the threat to his authority, the canny cardinal managed to turn the tables and manipulate events. Initially, Louis XIII ordered Richelieu's dismissal, but when he realized the extent of his mother's interference and intentions to exert control over him and his reign, the king reversed his decision, reaffirming support for Richelieu and leading to the downfall of Marie de' Medici and her allies. The former Queen of France died penniless in Cologne, Germany, in 1642, a mere five months before the cardinal himself followed her to the grave.

In terms of foreign policy, Richelieu pursued a pragmatic approach during the Thirty Years' War. This conflict spanned from 1618 to 1648 and engulfed much of Europe. Originating in the Holy Roman Empire, the war involved a complex web of religious, political, and territorial disputes. Initially ignited by tensions between Catholics and Protestants, the war was notorious for its shifting alliances and phases characterized by the intervention of external forces like France and Spain. The Peace of Westphalia in 1648 eventually brought an end to the conflict, marking a transformative moment in European geopolitics and solidifying the principle of *cuius regio, eius religio*, "Whosever territory, his religion"—allowing rulers to determine the religion of their respective territories.

France ended up playing a significant and somewhat paradoxical role in the conflict. Initially, despite the Catholic faith of the kingdom, Richelieu threw his support behind the Protestant states against the Habsburgs, but he later shifted alliances to maintain a delicate balance of power. Essentially, Richelieu pursued a realpolitik strategy, aiming to weaken the Habsburgs, traditional rivals of France, and enhance French power. Everything was done for the benefit of the French crown rather than for a moral or religious purpose, demonstrating the prioritization of national interests over religious affiliations. The French intervention, marked by financial and military support to Protestant states like Sweden, helped shift the balance of power in favor of the Protestant cause.

On the domestic front, Richelieu worked to fortify the economy and royal finances. His efforts included reducing the influence of private armies and dismantling fortified castles held by nobles, thereby mitigating potential threats to the crown. In the face of internal opposition from the likes of the king's own mother and brother, Richelieu adeptly navigated challenges, solidifying the monarchy's power. Beyond politics, Richelieu played a crucial role in fostering the arts and academia. As a patron of writers, artists, and intellectuals, he significantly contributed to the cultural and intellectual enrichment of France. His enduring legacy lies in shaping the French state, laying the groundwork for the absolute monarchy that would reach its zenith under Louis XIV. Despite facing criticism for his tactics, Richelieu's impact on French history is widely recognized as a transformative chapter in the evolution of the nation.

Though it was Louis XIII on the throne, it could be argued that it was the genius of Richelieu who initiated the state-building seen by the next king. When Richelieu died in 1642, France was a major European power, and he left it in the hands of his personally trained successor, Cardinal Jules Mazarin. About a year after Richelieu's passing, King Louis XIII also died, leaving his son, Louis XIV, to become the monarch at the tender age of four years and eight months.

Like Catherine and Marie before her, Louis XIII's wife and mother of the new king, Anne of Austria, became his regent. Power in the early days of Louis XIV's reign was mostly situated in the hands of his mother and Richelieu's protege, Cardinal Mazarin, and it was the latter who increasingly took charge.

Not long after Louis XIV's ascension to the throne, unrest rippled through the kingdom, with various nobles, government officials, and other discontented people expressing their dislike of the absolutist monarchy established under the current king's father and his minister. This discontent picked up steam, becoming a series of civil conflicts known as the Fronde. The first phase, or Parlementary Fronde, occurred within the space of a year from 1648 to 1649. Beginning, as the name suggests, within the Parlement of Paris, a judicial institution formed by Philip IV in the 1300s, this was a reaction to the monarchy's attempt to increase taxes and limit the Parlement's powers. Parlementaires sought to defend their traditional privileges and curb the royal reach, sparking street protests, various barricades, and a splash of mob violence. The Peace of Rueil in 1649 granted some concessions to the Parlement and temporarily stopped the unrest.

The following year, the second phase, or Fronde of the Princes, broke out, lasting until 1653. This focused largely on the nobility, particularly princes of the blood (*prince du sang*): the king's blood relatives, typically brothers and cousins, who had traditionally served as both political rivals and close advisors in years past. Irritated with Mazarin's centralization policies enacted on behalf of Louis XIV, the nobles sought to assert their influence and limit the king's control. Powerful nobles like the Prince de Condé and the Duke of Orléans were outspoken in their unhappiness. The Prince de Condé was particularly aggrieved, having assisted the monarchy during the Parlementary Fronde and failed to gain the political points he believed he earned.

Mazarin continued to be a target of rage during both the Parlementary Fronde and the Fronde of the Princes, with many despising his policies and influence over the young king. Condé managed to briefly hold the city of Paris, but his victory was short-lived as internal divisions within the nobility made their success fairly impossible. Condé fled, and Louis XIV re-entered Paris triumphantly on October 21, 1652, with his advisor Mazarin following suit in February. With many of the princes who had rebelled in exile, the power of the nobility was considerably checked. Furthermore, the Parlement was forbidden from intervening in royal affairs, allowing Mazarin's dream of absolutism to continue unabated. The Fronde was arguably a success for both Mazarin and the young Louis XIV. It was also the only significant challenge to royal power for the next century.

In 1661, the same year that Cardinal Mazarin passed away, Louis XIV assumed personal rule of France. Exactly one day after the death of his trusted advisor, Louis XIV informed all his ministers that he intended to take complete control of every aspect of governance. He saw himself as divinely appointed to rule and viewed any dissension from his will as a kind of sin. Known as the "Sun King," Louis XIV has become known as the ultimate example of an absolutist monarch in Europe and established one of the longest reigns in European history—remaining king until he died in 1715.

His rule was characterized by continuing the centralization of power initiated under Louis XIII and Richelieu and fostered by Mazarin in Louis XIV's youth. He famously declared, *L'état, c'est moi* ("I am the state"), epitomizing his fervent belief in absolute monarchy. Taking measures to diminish the influence of the nobility, Louis XIV removed the court from the power center of Paris and concentrated it instead at his royal palace of Versailles, roughly fifteen miles outside of the city. Here, he could more effectively control and monitor his courtiers, as well as make them dependent on him for entertainment, relevancy, and power.

Versailles[18] itself became a symbol of opulence and grandeur, a focal point of the king's reign. It served not only as a residence but also as a seat of government and a nerve center for cultural and political activities. Initially a humble hunting lodge owned by his father, Louis XIV envisioned transforming this modest abode into a symbol and statement of his royal authority. Enlisting the services of various architects like Louis Le Vau, Charles Le Brun, and André Le Nôtre, each contributed different aspects to the palace and grounds, with Le Vau designing the architecture, Le Brun overseeing the interior decoration, and Le Nôtre conceptualizing the extensive gardens. This list is not exhaustive, though— there were many other architects and artists responsible for forming the grandeur of Versailles.

The construction took place over several decades, with the first phase expanding the hunting lodge into a grand chateau with symmetrical wings. The iconic Hall of Mirrors, Grand Trianon, and Orangerie, as well as other structures, were all added during later phases. Le Nôtre's breathtakingly expansive gardens were characterized by geometric patterns, lavish fountains, and ornate statues. The landscaping became integral to the overall design, creating a harmonious blend of architecture and nature.

In 1682, the magnificent palace was at last complete. Louis XIV promptly uprooted his royal court from Paris and made Versailles the principal residence of the French monarchy. This ultimate status symbol of his absolutist rule was intended to both awe and impress visitors while reinforcing the king's authority.

Life at court was vivid and entertaining. To keep the nobles in line, Louis XIV strove to have them consistently occupied with gambling, gossip, performances, and an endless string of etiquette they were expected to follow. As a result, Louis XIV became a formidable patron of the arts, including literature, art, classical music, and dance, making France the cultural Mecca of Europe. Writers like Molière and Jean Racine were recipients of the king's generous patronage, though the financial support certainly came with strings, as they were instructed to only depict him and his rule in a flattering light.

Ballet, in particular, flourished under the Sun King. Brought to France a century earlier by the notorious Catherine de' Medici, Louis XIV was quite the passionate dancer himself. Of course, everything the king loved, his sycophants had to love, so ballet became a prevalent courtly art form. In 1661, he founded the Académie Royale de Danse, one of the earliest ballet schools, aiming to train professional dancers. Additionally, he established the Académie Royale de Musique (Royal Academy of Music), known today as the Paris Opera, which became a leading institution for ballet productions. Louis XIV's support and patronage helped elevate ballet to a refined and formalized art, influencing its development and establishing France as a center for balletic excellence in the European cultural landscape. Though long taken up by other nations, the art form still bears Louis XIV's mark—most ballet steps are all in the French language.

Though remembered for his impressive cultural contributions, not all of Louis XIV's royal actions are celebratory. His revocation of the Edict of Nantes in 1685 restricted religious freedoms for Protestants, stirred controversy, and had lasting repercussions for the future of France and its monarchy.

Aside from his domestic accomplishments, Louis XIV was a formidable opponent to other European monarchs, pursuing an ambitious agenda of territorial expansion and military conquest. Together with his minister, Jean-Baptiste Colbert, Louis XIV and France enjoyed a period of dominant hegemony on the European continent. One of the first targets of Louis XIV's desire to grow his empire was the Spanish Netherlands, which he believed to be the property of his wife, Maria Theresa of Spain. He invaded the region, leading to the War of Devolution from 1667 to 1668.

Essentially, Louis XIV sought to enforce a legal principle known as "devolution," which argued that the children from a first marriage had a claim to the inheritance of their mother's property before the children from her second marriage. In this case, Louis XIV claimed the Spanish-controlled territories in the Netherlands on behalf of his wife. Though the French forces performed well, a Triple Alliance of England, Sweden, and the Dutch Republic put pressure on the Sun King's efforts. The conflict was resolved with the Treaty of Aix-la-Chappelle in 1668, but this did not radically alter or shift the balance of power in Europe.

However, Louis XIV was not done with the Netherlands. Louis XIV's expansionist goals were on full display during the Dutch War from 1672 to 1678, sometimes referred to as the Franco-Dutch War. The Dutch Republic actively tried to resist French influence, irritating Louis XIV, who desperately wanted to increase dominance and territory in the region. French forces had several tactical victories, and the conflict ended with the Treaty of Nijmegen in 1678, which fell in favor of the French and damaged the Habsburg family's waning supremacy in Europe.

Louis XIV continued to campaign for French growth, forming a group of European powers interested in opposing his expansionist policies. The War of the League of Augsburg, also known as the Nine Years' War, lasted from 1688 to 1697 and concluded with the Treaty of Ryswick. This reaffirmed the territorial status quo with some minor changes. Louis XIV agreed to return certain territories to the Dutch and recognized William III of Orange as the legitimate ruler of England. This conflict drove home the idea that France could not continue to compete on the world stage completely alone; allies were increasingly necessary.

The final conflict of Louis XIV's reign was the War of the Spanish Succession, which lasted from 1701 to 1714 after Charles II of Spain died childless. The leading contenders for the inheritance were Archduke Charles of Austria, a grandson of Charles II, and Philip, Duke of Anjou, a grandson of King Louis XIV of France. The prospect of a single ruler controlling both the Spanish and French thrones raised concerns among other European powers about the potential for a dominant and powerful Bourbon monarchy.

Fought across multiple theaters, the war ended with the signing of the Treaty of Utrecht in 1713 and the Treaty of Rastatt in 1714. These treaties reshaped the European political landscape and recognized Philip of Anjou (now Philip V) as the legitimate king of Spain but stipulated that the French and Spanish crowns would remain separate to prevent the unification of the two powerful monarchies.

The reign of Louis XIV had a profound impact on France's political, cultural, and military landscape, solidifying the image of an absolute monarch and influencing subsequent European monarchies. The era also laid the groundwork for Enlightenment ideas and the challenges to absolute rule that would emerge in the eighteenth century. When he died in 1715, the monarchy was unpopular thanks to the lavish life the upper class led while the poor suffered in the streets. Since his sons and grandsons had preceded him in death, his successor was his five-year-old great-grandson. In his will, he attempted to leave power in the hands of his son by his former mistress, Madame de Montespan, due to his mistrust of his nephew, the Duke of Orléans, who would likely serve as regent otherwise.

The Parlement, long languishing in obscurity while the monarchy took the spotlight, nullified the will after he passed as a reminder of their potential political power. Louis XIV's successors could not recapture his absolute authority, and the stage for the Revolution at the end of the century was set.

Despite the efforts of his great-grandfather, the early reign of Louis XV, who ruled France from 1715 to 1774, was overseen by Philippe, Duke of Orléans. Serving as regent until Louis XV reached his majority in 1723, this period was marked by financial difficulties and military setbacks. Most of this was set in motion by the War of Spanish Succession, but real efforts to address fiscal issues and strengthen royal authority were met with resistance from multiple quarters, especially the various regional parlements (France's judicial bodies).

Louis XV, known as "the Beloved," had a long reign, but it was not full of victories for the French monarchy and instead was marked by a blend of political challenges, cultural developments, and diplomatic intrigues and intricacies. As the eighteenth century progressed, Great Britain rose in prominence, and France's hegemony faded. Conflicts like the War of Austrian Succession from 1740 to 1748 and the Seven Years' War from 1756 to 1763 had far-reaching consequences for European geopolitics and the health and future of the French economy. The Treaty of Paris that ended the Seven Years' War sealed the French crown's defeat. France ceded several important territories, like Canada, to the British Empire. This contributed to the formation of a financial crisis after the conclusion of Louis XV's reign that would significantly damage both the solvency and popularity of the French monarchy.

Even though France was failing on the world stage regarding military and economic achievements, the country remained a cultural hot spot for Europe, dictating much of the fashion, art, and philosophy that would come to dominate the continent. Louis XV's reign is often associated with the Rococo style, a decorative and ornate artistic sensibility known for its whimsical and charming characteristics. After years of the stately and formal Baroque style that had dominated the reign of the Sun King, the light-hearted, nature-based themes, asymmetry, intricate ornamentation, and pastel colors of Rococo works were a breath of fresh air. This can be seen in paintings like *The Swing*[19] (or *The Happy Accidents of the Swing*) by Jean-Honoré Fragonard and buildings like the Hôtel de Soubise[20] designed by Pierre-Alexis Delemair. This style eventually faded gently into Neoclassicism.

Aside from art and architecture, the salons of Paris were hotbeds of philosophical discourse. Figures like Voltaire and Jean-Jacques Rousseau were stars of the era, contributing to the intellectual climate that would influence the French Revolution in the latter half of the century.

Nevertheless, Louis XV's reign is often criticized for its perceived failures in governance, financial mismanagement, and the erosion of royal authority. The discontent and social inequalities that emerged during this time laid the groundwork for the more tumultuous period that followed. Though referred to as the "Beloved" in the early days of his reign, the missteps and defeats suffered by France during his tenure as monarch earned him the disdain and derision of his subjects. When he went to his grave in 1774, the French people mourned his passing no more than they had that of his predecessor.

Louis XV's son died about a decade before, leaving royal power in the hands of his twenty-year-old grandson, now crowned Louis XVI. As the last reigning monarch of France prior to the Revolution, he inherited the struggles of his three-time great-grandfather and his grandfather. Thus, his rule was marred by economic challenges, fiscal mismanagement, and social unrest. The financial strain on the country caused growing discontent, exacerbated by France's involvement in the American Revolutionary War. In addition to the expense of aiding the Americans, the monarchy's extravagant lifestyle and resistance to any type of reform in that arena fueled popular distaste and dislike for their monarchs. Hate for the king was growing, and his controversial wife did not aid matters.

Marie Antoinette, born Maria Antonia Josepha Johanna, was an Archduchess of Austria and the last Queen of France before the French Revolution. She married Louis XVI of France in 1770 at the age of fourteen as part of an alliance between Austria and France. Criticism for her supposed extravagant lifestyle and perceived interference in politics caused her reputation to suffer. How much of Marie Antoinette's reputation rests in fact or fiction remains lost to history and is colored by the events surrounding and following her fall from grace. The famous phrase, "Let them eat cake," was likely not spoken by her at all and is believed to be a misrepresentation of the young queen.

In May 1789, a financial crisis led to the convening of the Estates-General, a meeting of the three estates of France: the clergy, the nobility, and the commons. However, the representatives of the Third Estate (the common people) broke away, forming the National Assembly and initiating a series of events that led to the storming of the Bastille on July 14, 1789, marking the beginning of the French Revolution. The Bastille, a fortress and state prison in Paris, became a symbol of royal tyranny, and its storming represented a symbolic act of defiance against the oppressive monarchy and a declaration of the people's quest for freedom.

As tensions escalated, Louis XVI grew worried for his and his family's safety, and he attempted to flee Paris with them in June 1791 and gain the protection of his wife's family in

Austria. The royal family was apprehended in Varennes, about one hundred and fifty miles outside of Paris, damaging the king's credibility in the eyes of the public. A little over a year later, the monarchy was officially abolished, and France became a republic. Louis XVI was arrested, tried for high treason, and convicted. He was executed by guillotine on January 21, 1793, marking a pivotal moment in the French Revolution. His wife was arrested and tried as well. Found guilty of treason and other charges, she followed her husband to the guillotine some months later, meeting her end on October 16, 1793, at the Place de la Révolution in Paris.

Of the couple's four children, only one survived. Two had already died prior to the Revolution, and the heir-apparent, Louis-Charles, passed in 1795 at age ten, likely due to complications from tuberculosis. Their eldest daughter, Marie-Thérèse, married the Duke of Angoulême in 1799. She lived the rest of her life caught up in the drama of her and her husband's noble blood. She died in 1851 in the Austrian Empire. The reign and fate of Louis XVI and Marie Antoinette became emblematic of the profound political and social transformations of the era.

Even with the elimination of the monarchy, the bloodshed in France was not done. The Reign of Terror, which had commenced in September 1793, was still in its early days when the guillotine dropped onto Marie Antoinette's neck. The streets of Paris had yet more blood to spill.

9

LIBERTY, FRATERNITY, EQUALITY... OR DEATH (1789–1906 CE)

With hindsight, the French Revolution or some similar outpouring of change coupled with violence seems inevitable. The Revolution, spanning from 1789 to 1799, was driven by a convergence of political, social, and economic factors. A severe financial crisis stemmed from accumulated debt, incurred mainly during wars—particularly the American Revolutionary War—and by extravagant spending by the monarchy. Social inequality was exacerbated by centuries of the feudal system, which privileged the clergy and nobility while burdening the lower classes with unequal taxation. Furthermore, Enlightenment ideas advocating individual rights, liberty, and equality, as championed by popular thinkers like Rousseau and Voltaire, inspired a widespread questioning of existing social and political structures.

Political unrest ensued due to weak leadership under King Louis XVI, whose indecisiveness and inability to address the financial crisis created a power vacuum. The outdated administrative and financial systems of the Bourbon monarchy proved ineffective in the face of contemporary challenges. Food shortages resulting from crop failures and harsh winters led to widespread suffering among the lower classes and fueled events like the Women's March on Versailles in 1789 that protested the high cost of bread.

After the formation of the National Assembly and the Storming of the Bastille, the revolutionary spirit found expression in the Declaration of the Rights of Man and of the Citizen, a seminal document that enshrined the principles of equality, liberty, and fraternity. At first, it seemed that the Bourbons might survive the unrest, though their power was sharply curtailed with the establishment of a constitutional monarchy in 1791. However, the revolutionary fervor escalated into a radical phase characterized by the abolition of the monarchy. This was exemplified by the execution of King Louis XVI in 1793 and the ascendance of the Jacobins, a radical political group advocating for republican ideals, social equality, and the use of revolutionary measures. Led by Maximilien Robespierre, the Jacobins played a central role in the escalation of violence and the inception of the Reign of Terror in 1793.

Robespierre and his compatriots' fervent beliefs took control of the Committee of Public Safety, the provisional government put in place following the abolition of the monarchy. Beginning in 1793, the members of the Committee of Public Safety, particularly Robespierre, pushed a period of extreme political violence known as the Reign of Terror. Lasting from 1793 to 1794, this was marked by mass executions of perceived enemies of the Revolution. Thousands were killed, mostly by the guillotine, in an attempt to eliminate any counter-revolutionary forces lurking in the nation.

Unfortunately for Robespierre, he fell victim to the same violence he perpetuated in the end. During July 1794, fears of arbitrary arrests and executions prompted a coalition of moderates and former revolutionaries to orchestrate Robespierre's arrest. Bolstered by the growing public dissatisfaction with Robespierre and the Committee of Public Safety, he was executed on July 28 of the same year, symbolizing a definite end to the more radical phase of the French Revolution.

What followed was the Thermidorian Reaction, named for the month of Thermidor in the French Republican Calendar. Thermidorian leaders sought to restore political stability, ease economic hardships, and move towards a more moderate form of government, returning to the ideals of the early revolutionary days and espousing the ideals of free markets and freedom of religion. However, the Thermidorians were hardly a united group. Though more conservative, some sought the return of the constitutional monarchy while others preferred a more moderate republic than the Jacobins had been intent on creating. During their rise to prominence, many Jacobins were forcibly removed from power and violently ended. The White Terror in 1795 was a prime example, with mass arrests, trials, and executions of Jacobins, both confirmed and suspected.

Life for the average Frenchman and woman was no better under the Thermidorians than it had been under the Jacobins and the Bourbons before them. The formation of the Directory after the Thermidorian Reaction, unfortunately, proved to be more of the same. Operating as the governing body of France from 1795 to 1799, the political landscape during the Directory was characterized by a struggle for power among various political factions. The government was comprised of five Directors, and it faced criticism for its perceived corruption and ineffectiveness. Economic difficulties, including high inflation and food shortages, further undermined public support.

The Directory contended with internal rebellions from both the Jacobin left and the Royalist right, such as the Prairial Uprising and the Revolt of 13 Vendémiaire in 1795. Additionally, external threats from other European monarchies who sought to contain the revolutionary ideals emanating from France threatened the security of the new nation. The War of the First Coalition, a struggle between the French and the combined pro-monarchy forces of Austria, Prussia, Great Britain, the Dutch Republic, and Spain, had been an ongoing conflict since the outset of the Revolution as other European nations sought to contain what they saw as a rebellious contagion within France.

Militarily, France hit its stride under the command of a young Corsican general named Napoléon Bonaparte. Leading the Italian Campaign between 1796 and 1797, Napoléon's achievements on the Italian Peninsula contributed significantly to his reputation as a military genius. Napoléon's forces enjoyed victories against Austrian and Sardinian forces at battles like Lodi, Arcole, and Rivoli, often employing innovative tactics and utilizing speed and flexibility. He often showcased brilliance in his ability to outmaneuver larger and more traditional armies, befuddling his opponents and dazzling his supporters.

The Treaty of Campo Formio in 1797 concluded the Italian campaign, securing territorial gains for France and redrawing the political map of Europe. He continued to distinguish himself during the War of the Second Coalition that kicked off the following year and lasted until 1802. This was another attempt by major European powers like Great Britain, the Holy Roman Empire, Russia, the Ottoman Empire, and Portugal to check France's military and intellectual spread into the rest of the continent. Major events included the Egyptian campaign led by Napoléon, where he sought to disrupt British access to India and bolster France's trade with the Levant area. The coalition enjoyed some success, with the British Navy under Rear-Admiral Sir Horatio Nelson dealing French forces a defeat at the Battle of the Nile in 1798. Despite initial successes, internal strife and shifting alliances weakened the coalition, and the war ultimately ended with a French victory and the establishment of the Treaty of Amiens in 1802, providing a brief respite before hostilities resumed.

This success elevated Napoléon's status in France and set the stage for his further military and political ambitions, ultimately leading to his rise to power as First Consul and later Emperor. The internal conflicts, economic woes, and overall political instability of the Directory created an environment ripe for a coup d'état, which was realized by Napoléon in 1799.

Known as the Coup of 1 Brumaire, on November 9, 1799, Napoléon led a coup that dissolved the existing government of the Directory and established a new one under his control. Named the Consulate, it was a new executive authority in control of the country, and Napoléon became the First Consul, holding the reigns to executive power in France. Interested in first stabilizing the country, Napoléon implemented a series of reforms that targeted the economic and political variability that had plagued France for some time. To scrounge up money for his nation, Napoléon sold the entirety of France's colonial holdings on the North American continent to the nascent United States in 1803 in an act known as the Louisiana Purchase. Divesting France of this lucrative piece of land may not have been the best long-term move, but it provided him with much-needed funds and gave him the room to turn his attention inward and reform France. Chief among these reforms was the Napoléonic Code.

Established in 1804, the Napoléonic Code, officially known as the Civil Code of the French, was a comprehensive legal system that aimed to consolidate and modernize the diverse laws existing in France before the French Revolution. The code prioritized clarity and coherence, emphasizing principles such as equality before the law, protection of private property, and the restriction of privileges based on birth. Its influence extended beyond France, serving as a model for legal systems in many countries, like Italy and Spain, and contributing to the development of civil law traditions around the world.

However, Napoléon's pretense as a man of liberty and Enlightenment ideals was somewhat short-lived. By 1804, the same year he introduced the Napoléonic Code, he crowned himself Emperor of the French at an elaborate ceremony attended by the current pontiff, Pope Pius VII. This act was reminiscent of the monarchs of old, traditionally crowned by the pope as Charlemagne was in 800 CE.

However, his refusal to allow Pius VII to coronate him represented a consolidation of power in his hands, with no one on heaven or earth to control him.

Despite jettisoning France's North American holdings to the United States, Napoléon was interested in expanding his French Empire, particularly on the European continent. Internationally, Napoléon embarked on a series of military campaigns that put his military genius on full display and frightened his geopolitical neighbors. After the Wars of the First and Second Coalition solved little for the tension on the European continent, another conflict was soon at hand. Known as the Napoléonic Wars from 1803 to 1815, they featured a series of conflicts between Napoléon's French Empire and various coalitions of European powers.

The key phases of the Napoléonic Wars included the War of the Third Coalition, marked by Napoléon's triumph at Austerlitz against the Russian and Austrian Empires in 1805, and the War of the Fourth Coalition from 1806 to 1807, during which victories at Jena and Auerstedt against Prussia and Saxony led to the establishment of the Confederation of the Rhine. This group of German client states united at Napoléon's behest, replacing the Holy Roman Empire and including a coalition of German states under French influence. The member states, situated mainly in the western and southwestern parts of the German-speaking region, pledged their allegiance to Napoléon and were granted a degree of autonomy.

Violence raged on with the Peninsular War (1808–1814), witnessing conflicts in the Iberian Peninsula against British and Spanish forces, which created strains on French

174 | DOMINIC HAYNES

resources. The Invasion of Russia in 1812 proved disastrous for Napoléon as he marched his troops ever deeper into the intensifying Russian winter, stretching his supply lines dubiously thin and weakening his forces significantly. The War of the Sixth Coalition (1813–1814) saw a mass of allied forces like Great Britain, Russia, Austria, Prussia, Sweden, Saxony, and Mecklenburg-Schwerin coming together to defeat Napoléon at the Battle of Leipzig—also known as the Battle of the Nations—and invade France. The loss at Leipzig and the failed invasion of Russia were humiliating, and Napoléon could not politically survive. Forced to abdicate as part of the Treaty of Fontainebleau in 1814, he was exiled to Elba, a small Mediterranean island off the coast of Tuscany. Louis XVIII, the younger brother of the late King Louis XVI, assumed the French throne, briefly restoring the Bourbon family to the monarchy.

In March 1815, Napoléon escaped from Elba and staged a dramatic return to power in France, regaining control during a frantic period known as the Hundred Days. However, this was no lasting rule, and much of Napoléon's luck was gone. He took to the battlefield again a few months after his return at the Battle of Waterloo. Standing alone against the military might of Great Britain under Arthur Wellesley, the Duke of Wellington, and his various Belgian, Prussian, and German allies, Napoléon was soundly defeated and forced to abdicate once more.

This time, he declared his young son Napoléon II as his successor, though this was never formally recognized and the boy remained in Austria with his mother for the duration of his supposed reign. As for the famed emperor and general, Napoléon was exiled from France once more, sentenced to live out his days on the remote British-controlled island of St. Helena in the middle of the Atlantic Ocean. He died there in 1821, succumbing to stomach cancer.

The reign of Napoléon and the ensuing Napoléonic Wars changed the political makeup of Europe, contributing to the rise of nationalism, alterations in borders, and the establishment of the Concert of Europe—a collection of the continent's monarchies interested in maintaining stability, preserving the status quo, and keeping separate spheres of influence. In a few words, the Concert of Europe existed to prevent the rise of another Napoléon. This would be strongly tested in the following century.

With Napoléon removed from the public eye, the Bourbon family was once more placed on the throne of France, setting off a fifteen-year period known as the Bourbon Restoration. Louis XVIII was once more declared king, and a constitutional monarchy was established under his rule. However, it would be folly to think that all the upheaval of the last several decades would allow a Bourbon king to return to the throne with no friction. Naturally, the restoration faced challenges: lingering dissatisfaction among the populace and opposition from both conservative and liberal factions. The monarchy struggled to reconcile with the revolutionary ideals that had shaped France and grappled with royalists who wanted a full-scale return to the *ancien régime* of old and liberals who pushed for constitutional reforms.

In 1824, Louis XVIII died childless, and the crown passed to his brother, Charles X, a fervent royalist. Bent on increasing royal power and limiting liberal reforms, his reign grew increasingly unpopular among the public, culminating with the July Revolution of 1830. Triggered by a combination of political, social, and economic grievances, it resulted in the overthrow of the Bourbon monarchy under Charles X. The final catalyst for the uprising was Charles X's decision to issue the July Ordinances, which restricted civil liberties and altered the electoral system in favor of the aristocracy.

Public outrage and opposition to these measures led to widespread protests in Paris. The conflict escalated in the latter half of July. Street battles ensued, and the revolutionaries seized control of key points in the city. Charles X abdicated in favor of his grandson, Henry V, but this successor was rejected. Instead, the July Monarchy was established. Louis-Philippe, the Duke of Orléans and a descendant of King Louis XIII, became the "Citizen King." The tricolor flag of blue, white, and red was reinstated, censorship was abolished, the voting age was dropped to twenty-five, and the property qualification was lowered to encompass those who paid a tax of two hundred francs instead of the former quantity of three hundred. This essentially doubled the number of eligible French voters from about ninety thousand to nearly two hundred thousand.

The July Revolution marked a shift towards a constitutional monarchy, but it did not fully address the social and economic issues. Despite the initial optimism and reforms, Louis-Philippe's reign faced challenges, and the period witnessed further political unrest leading up to the Revolutions of 1848. Essentially, Louis-Philippe had been largely supported by the upper-class bourgeoisie, and though his ascension to the throne seemed like a victory for the common folk over the nobility, he failed to garner the support of the growing lower industrial classes in France.

The mechanization of industries, particularly the textile sector, as well as the growth and development of the rail, coal, and iron industries, drove the Industrial Revolution in the country, pushing people from rural villages and farms into urban centers. However, like any seismic shift in humanity's way of life, these changes sparked debates on social inequality, labor conditions, and what role the state had to play in the lives of its citizens. Louis-Philippe and the shaky July Monarchy were ill-equipped to answer these challenging queries.

The economic and industrial developments, coupled with new social and political tension, led to greater calls for political participation and social justice. French citizens remained, understandably, unsatisfied with their lots in life and pushed for revolution once more. This snowballed into the February Revolution of 1848. Widespread discontent over economic hardships, high food prices, and political corruption sparked a series of protests and barricades in Paris on February 22, and Louis-Philippe ultimately abdicated, naming his grandson Louis-Philippe II as his successor. This wish was disregarded by the political leaders of the time. Instead, a provisional government was established, and the Second Republic of France was declared.

The revolution did indeed bring significant social and political changes. Universal male suffrage was introduced, and a right-to-work was established, charging the government to provide all citizens with jobs. However, once again, liberal and conservative factions found themselves at odds with how to govern their new republic. Socialist thinkers pushed for increasingly liberal benefits and reforms, while conservative thinkers worked to quash these ideas. During the summer of 1848, workers' uprisings were violently suppressed by the ruthless conservative General Cavaignac, and the more radical leanings of the revolution were effectively dismantled.

A new constitution was drawn up in November 1848, and Louis-Napoléon Bonaparte, the nephew of Napoléon Bonaparte, was elected as the first President of the Second Republic. Much like his illustrious uncle, Louis-Napoléon was not satisfied with this lot in life. On December 2, 1851, he orchestrated a coup, dissolving the National Assembly, dismissing the Council of Ministers, and declaring a state of emergency. He deployed troops throughout Paris to suppress any vestiges of resistance and followed all of this with a constitutional referendum that pushed major power into his hands as the executive power of the nation. After the new constitution was approved in January of 1852, Louis-Napoléon became Emperor Napoléon III exactly one year after his fateful coup. The Second French Empire proved to be a time of relative stability for France, though it did end the republican experiment initiated by the Revolution of 1848.

During his reign, Napoléon III pursued policies to modernize France and consolidate his regime's power, embracing significant economic, infrastructural, and cultural developments. Napoléon III, influenced by ideas of social stability and order, implemented public works projects such as the renovation of Paris by Georges-Eugène Haussmann. This transformation included the creation of broad boulevards in lieu of cramped and winding medieval streets, parks like the Bois de Boulogne, and improved sanitation via a sewer system.

Napoléon III also sought to enhance France's international standing within Europe and beyond. For years, France had faced multiple European coalitions on its own. However, under Napoléon III, a shift occurred in its foreign policy. From 1853 to 1856, France actively participated in the Crimean War, joining forces with other major powers, including its longstanding adversary, Great Britain. The alliance's primary goal was to curb the territorial ambitions of the Russian Empire in the Black Sea area and to safeguard religious rights in the Holy Land. This coalition managed to defeat Russia, keeping the Black Sea area neutral and open.

He involved France more deeply abroad as well, colonizing a portion of Asia that includes present-day Vietnam, Laos, and Cambodia. The country's efforts in Asia would continue well into the twentieth century, proving to be a drain on France and devastating to the local Asian areas they exploited.

Unfortunately, Napoléon III's extended international involvement became quite expensive. The Crimean War, the colonization efforts in Asia, the Franco-Austrian War in 1859, and the ultimately fruitless French efforts to establish a client state in Mexico under a Habsburg prince during the 1860s all put a strain on France's resources. The latter portion of Napoléon III's reign faced mounting political opposition and economic challenges. This was further intensified by the Franco-Prussian War beginning in 1870. It seemed France was interested in renewing its reputation as the preeminent power on the European continent, but this was no longer the case.

The Prussian military, equipped with advanced weaponry and led by generals such as Helmuth von Moltke, proved highly effective. The French suffered defeats, including the pivotal Battle of Sedan, leading to the humiliating capture of Napoléon III. The war culminated in the Siege of Paris and the establishment of the German Empire in 1871. The Treaty of Frankfurt concluded the conflict, resulting in territorial losses for France, notably the ceding of Alsace and Lorraine to the newly formed German state.

Following Napoléon III's capture by the Germans, he was deposed in absentia, and a Third Republic of France was declared. This got off to a rough start when the Paris Commune was formed in 1871—a radical socialist and revolutionary government that briefly took control of the city of Paris. Characterized by its progressive policies, including worker self-management, separation of church and state, and other social reforms, it faced strong opposition from conservative and republican forces alike. The Third Republic, led by Adolphe Thiers, launched a military assault on the Commune in May 1871, resulting in its brutal suppression.

Ultimately, despite its rocky start, the Third Republic of France was the political regime that governed the country from 1870 to 1940 and navigated numerous challenges during its existence, including political divisions, social upheavals, economic struggles, and external conflicts. Mostly, the Third Republic worked to modernize the nation through social and educational reforms while grappling with various anti-republican sentiments from monarchists who wanted a return to the absolutism of the kings and nationalists who saw the Republic as too moderate and conservative.

The republic faced significant crises, such as the Dreyfus Affair, a divisive controversy surrounding the wrongful conviction of a Jewish military officer named Alfred Dreyfus. The scandal lasted from 1894 into 1906 and centered around Dreyfus being falsely accused of passing military secrets to the German Empire. Convicted of treason in a secret military court-martial based on flimsy evidence, Dreyfus's ordeal exposed highly polarized and deep divisions within French society, pitting anti-Semitic and nationalist factions against those advocating for justice and human rights. Emile Zola's famous open letter titled *J'Accuse...!* charged the French government with anti-Semitism and a gross miscarriage of justice.

When Dreyfus's innocence was revealed, he was retried in 1899. Despite the revelation that another officer, Ferdinand Walsin Esterhazy, was the real culprit, anti-Semitism and negative sentiments toward Dreyfus continued. He was eventually fully exonerated in 1906, but the affair had a lasting impact on French politics and society, contributing to increased awareness of anti-Semitism and calls for justice and civil liberties.

Along with continued involvement in Asia with the formation of French Indochina in 1887, France also delved further into matters on the African continent. The late nineteenth century was not the first time France had been involved in Africa—the country had invaded Algeria in the 1830s during the reign of Louis-Philippe. During the 1880s, France began expanding into Tunisia and Morocco in North Africa and pushed into West Africa as well, building colonies in what would become the nations of Senegal, Mali, Burkina Faso, Benin, and more. French expeditions also explored and claimed territories in Central Africa, establishing the French Congo. Chief among the reasons for invading these regions was the so-called "civilizing" concerns called the Mission Civilisatrice or "civilizing mission," which asserted that French colonization brought Christianity and culture to those who needed it.

Furthermore, France was keen to assert its dominance among other European powers who used their colonies to bolster their own prestige and wealth. In reality, colonization was driven by an exploitation of the economic potential of Africa. Resources like rubber, palm oil, minerals, and agricultural products were advantageous to France, and new colonies provided a market for French goods.

The late nineteenth century in France is often called the *Belle Époque* (Beautiful Era). Marked by economic prosperity, cultural flourishing, and innovations in art, literature, and technology, this was a welcome change from all the unrest and drama that preceded the Third Republic. The relative economic growth and political stability, coupled with the expansion of industrialization, led to increased production and wealth. A middle class sprang up and, with it, a consumer culture. There was time now for art and the consumption of it. Notable figures like Marcel Proust and Émile Zola led the way in literature, while artists like Claude Monet, Paul Cézanne, and Émile Gallé pioneered Impressionism, Post-Impressionism, and Art Nouveau, respectively. Theater and cabarets became popular arenas for entertainment, like the notorious Moulin Rouge. Distinctive fashion trends took off, particularly for women, showcasing hourglass silhouettes, elaborate hats, and corsets, providing a visual signal that social norms were shifting and women's societal roles were evolving.

Science and technology were booming—the Eiffel Tower was constructed for the Exposition Universelle in 1889 and became the new symbol for modern Paris. Scientists like Marie and Pierre Curie pushed forward groundbreaking work. Furthermore, the introduction of automobiles and advancements in aviation reflected the spirit of progress, heralding the dawn of a new age. By the end of the nineteenth century, Paris had become a cultural hub that attracted artists, writers, intellectuals, and musicians worldwide, contributing to its reputation as the "City of Light." All seemed well, but sadly, the Belle Époque was a brief golden age before the disruptions and horrors of the twentieth century. Trouble was on the horizon, and France's youth would be bathed in blood again.

10

A CENTURY OF BRUTALITY:
FRANCE IN THE MODERN AGE
(1894–2023 CE)

The early days of the twentieth century were a slow build-up of pre-existing tensions on the European continent. France, alone for much of the nineteenth century, sought alliances to protect the nation and avoid isolation. First came the Franco-Russian alliance in 1894, and then the *Entente Cordiale* with Great Britain in 1904. Britain allied with Russia, as well, with the Anglo-Russian Entente in 1907, and ultimately, the trio of France, Great Britain, and Russia formed the Triple Entente during the same year. France still contended with anti-Anglo sentiment and remained less than enthused to be allied with their old English enemies but conceded that the threat posed by the rising German state necessitated friendship with Britannia.

These three nations were not alone in their efforts to establish relationships with other powers, and the Triple Entente was formed in response to the existence of other alliances on the continent. Germany and Austria-Hungary had a long friendship and had been allied since 1879. Germany essentially offered Austria-Hungary a "blank check" of unconditional support. Italy was also loosely involved in this agreement, forming the Triple Alliance in 1882. The three countries periodically renewed the terms of their alliance, though France and Italy also reached a separate agreement that each would remain neutral should the other be attacked.

This complex web of alliances ensured that should one entity in Europe attack another, the whole continent would be drawn into confusion and, potentially, conflict. Furthermore, the increasing nationalism, imperialism, and militarism throughout the latter half of the nineteenth and the early half of the twentieth century turned Europe into a tinderbox that was simply awaiting a match.

On June 28, 1914, that flame was fatefully struck. Archduke Franz Ferdinand, the heir to the Austro-Hungarian throne, and his wife, Sophie, were shot and killed during a visit to Sarajevo, Bosnia. These bullets were fired by Gavrilo Princip, a member of a Serbian nationalist group called the Black Hand, who was motivated by the desire for the independence of South Slavic peoples from Austro-Hungarian rule. Austria-Hungary, seeking to address perceived Serbian involvement in the assassination, issued an ultimatum to Serbia, which triggered a domino effect leading to World War I. Serbia had an agreement with Russia, so when Austria-Hungary moved on the Serbs, Russia—and later, by extension, the Triple Entente—answered.

On the other side, Austria-Hungary called in the blank check offered by Germany. Italy declared neutrality, but the

Ottoman Empire and Bulgaria joined the conflict on Germany's side and formed the Central Powers. Italy and the United States ultimately joined the conflict on the side of the Allied Powers of Great Britain, France, and Russia, but they were not present for the initial fighting.

Diplomatic efforts on all sides failed, armies were swiftly mobilized, and World War I, also known as the Great War, broke out in 1914, one month after the death of Franz Ferdinand. As a multi-front war, several theaters developed in the early days of the conflict, mostly the Eastern and Western Fronts on either side of Germany. Before the outset of the conflict, Germany had developed the Schlieffen Plan, developed by Count Alfred von Schlieffen, who saw the Franco-Russian Alliance in the late 1800s as a guarantee that Germany could face a two-front war. This plan made two assumptions—firstly, that Russia would be slow to mobilize and attack in Germany's east, and secondly, that France was militarily weak and unprepared for the German forces.

Schlieffen proposed that Germany move swiftly on France, enacting a rapid and overwhelming offensive through neutral Belgium that would avoid the fortified Franco-German border, encircle Paris, and force a quick surrender. That way, the western threat to Germany would be neutralized before Russia mobilized, giving the nation time to turn its attention to the east and deal with Russia when they were ready. Ultimately, this did not work out the way the German military minds imagined it: the invasion of Belgium triggered Great Britain's entry into the war, and the rapid movement of German troops proved challenging. The combined forces of Britain and France put up a much stronger resistance than Germany had planned, and rather than a quick victory in the west, Germany faced a protracted and painful conflict, dooming them to fight a war in the east and the west simultaneously.

At the outset of the war in 1914, both Allied and Central Powers expected a more mobile conflict. However, the German advance was halted at the Battle of the Marne in September, leading to a stalemate and the beginning of trench warfare. After the Marne, both sides attempted to outflank the other in what became known as the "Race to the Sea," initiating the construction of a continuous line of trenches from the English Channel to Switzerland as both sides sought to secure their positions. Though the word "trench" suggests a simple ditch for hiding, the Western Front evolved into a complex system that utilized multiple layers and levels of trenches, barbed wire, and elaborate fortifications, forcing soldiers into harsh conditions characterized by near-constant mud and disease, not to mention the looming threat of the enemy's artillery and sniper fire.

Furthermore, technology in World War I far outpaced tactics. The introduction of tanks, poison gas, and more sophisticated artillery marked attempts to break the grueling deadlock. Still, these innovations offered no decisive breakthrough and only served to make the conflict more deadly and horrifying. The Battles of Verdun and the Somme, both in 1916, were particularly brutal and resulted in enormous casualties on both sides. By 1918, the arrival of fresh Allied Troops from the United States kicked off a series of successful offensives. The Hundred Days Offensive began in August and ultimately broke the German resistance, leading to the signing of the Armistice in November 1918.

France, in particular, was devastated by World War I. The Western Front, where much of the war was fought, extended chiefly across northern France. Over one hundred years after the conclusion of the Great War, the pockmarks of trenches and craters from explosives still dot the land around the Somme and Verdun. With the stalemate in the trenches, World War I devolved into a horrifying war of attrition that ground down individuals in the same way it sought to grind down a nation. France suffered immense human losses, and among the Allied Powers, only Russia, with its massive population and inferior technology, outpaced France for military casualties.

The signing of the Armistice on November 11, 1918 marked the end of hostilities. Signed in a railway carriage in Compiègne Forest in France, the date is now commemorated as Armistice Day or Remembrance Day. The static nature of the Front and the high casualties incurred enacted a lasting impact on the collective memory of France that was not to be easily forgiven or forgotten.

To lay the conflict to rest, the major powerbrokers of the Allies convened at Versailles, specifically inside the famed Hall of Mirrors, to negotiate the terms. Important figures present were President Woodrow Wilson of the United States, Prime Minister David Lloyd George of Great Britain, Prime Minister Georges Clemenceau of France, and Prime Minister Vittorio Orlando of Italy. The "Big Four," as they were called, did all the negotiations without any input from the Central Powers, though it was chiefly America, Great Britain, and France who were the architects of the treaty. Harsh terms were imposed on Germany, including territorial losses and financial reparations.

In greater detail, Germany lost Alsace-Lorraine to France and West Prussia to Poland. The Saar Basin, Germany's chief source of coal, was placed under the administration of the newly formed League of Nations, and German colonies in Africa and the Pacific were distributed among the Allied Powers. Severe restrictions on the size and capabilities of the German military were enacted, prohibiting the existence of an air force, tanks, and submarines. Germany was also required to pay financial reparations to the Allied Powers for damage caused during the war, creating a substantial economic burden for a nation already crippled by war and defeat. The Allied Powers also placed full responsibility for the war on the German nation and its allies in Article 231 of the treaty. This "war guilt clause" became a source of deep bitterness for Germans in the interwar years.

The Treaty of Versailles also established the League of Nations, an international organization to prevent future conflicts. Seen as the predecessor of the United Nations, the League of Nations was ultimately not as powerful as it could have been since the United States refused to join, weakening its overall effectiveness. The punitive measures of the Treaty of Versailles are often criticized for contributing to the economic and political instability of Germany, which eventually played a role in the rise of Adolf Hitler and the outbreak of World War II. Debates over the treaty's impact and whether the terms were too harsh continue into the present.

Despite the Allied victory, the interwar period in France (1918–1939) saw profound economic challenges such as inflation, unemployment, and financial strain, making it all the more difficult to stabilize and recover from the widespread devastation inflicted during the Great War. Politically, France experienced a period of instability characterized by the formation of multiple governments and oscillations between left and right-wing coalitions. Additionally, the Treaty of Versailles caused friction among political factions at home in France and abroad between the Allied Powers. Some believed the terms were too harsh and that Germany would never get back on its feet, while others thought the terms were merited due to the severity of the Great War. As a political whole, France typically offered no sympathy to the beleaguered German state, and this caused friction with its allies from time to time.

Germany had a hard time meeting the payments for the reparations. In 1923, France and Belgium occupied the Ruhr region in response to Germany's perceived non-compliance with the reparation payments. Eventually, through the Dawes Plan, the United States loaned the nation money and reduced Germany's current payments, allowing for them to be increased as the country's economy strengthened. The French president, Raymond Poincaré, accepted this arrangement, and France moved back out of the Ruhr in 1925.

Despite the economic and political challenges, the interwar years were a prosperous time for creativity, art, literature, and intellectual pursuits. The "Roaring Twenties" saw a brief but wild economic boom that bolstered French society, nurturing artistic movements like Cubism, Surrealism, and Dadaism. Creative giants of the twentieth century, like Pablo Picasso[21], André Breton[22], and Marcel Duchamp, found refuge within the confines of post-war Paris.

However, the global Great Depression in the late 1920s and early 1930s exacerbated economic difficulties in France, contributing to social unrest and political dissatisfaction. It was not Germany alone that saw the rise of fascism. This political movement reverberated across Europe, and France was no exception. Far-right movements like Action Française, founded by Charles Maurras, sparked concerns about the spread of authoritarianism. While some argue whether or not Action Française was truly fascist, it certainly had authoritarian and anti-democratic elements that impacted French political thought, though France never succumbed to an internally-led fascist regime.

The 1930s were a difficult time globally, and that, coupled with the aftermath of World War I, fed directly into the inception of World War II. The alliances, though familiar, were slightly altered by the end of the 1930s. In the beginning, France was counted alongside Great Britain and the Soviet Union as the primary Allied Powers. The United States joined after Pearl Harbor in 1941 on the side of the Allies. On the other side were the Axis Powers of Nazi Germany, Italy, and Japan. The unresolved issues left by World War I, coupled with economic instability and the rise of aggressive totalitarian regimes like Hitler's Germany and Mussolini's Italy, made conflict, once more, unavoidable.

In 1939, Hitler invaded Poland in a bid for territorial expansion, prompting the Allied Powers to swiftly declare war on Germany. Once again, Germany faced a two-front war, and similar to the initial intention of the Schlieffen Plan, German military leaders opted to move quickly. Employing the Blitzkrieg tactic, characterized by fast-moving armored units and air support, several European countries were conquered in quick succession, chief among them France in 1940.

The *Blitzkrieg* tactics first seen in Poland at the outset of the war were deployed in France the following year. French and Allied forces were swiftly defeated, resulting in the evacuation of what remained of the French and British troops from Dunkirk in June 1940. Following the German victory, a collaborationist government known as Vichy France led by Marshal Philippe Pétain was established in the southern part of the country. Though formally still "at war" with Germany and refusing to join the Axis Powers, Vichy France was, in truth, cooperating with the Nazis and their designs. Anti-Semitic policies were introduced, like the *Statut des Juifs* (Statute of the Jews), which sharply restricted the rights of Jewish citizens. Furthermore, political opposition was suppressed, and contributions to the German war effort were encouraged.

The northern portion of France, including the city of Paris, remained under direct occupation by Nazi German forces. The occupiers established a military administration to control the region, and the French population faced restrictions, curfews, and harsh living conditions. Scores of French Jews were arrested and deported to various concentration and extermination camps throughout Germany and Poland. The most infamous incident was the Velodrome d'Hiver (Vel' d'Hiv) Roundup in July 1942, where French authorities, with German assistance, arrested and deported thousands of Jews.

Germany exploited France's resources, industries, and agricultural production for its war effort. The Germans heavily regulated the French economy, and French workers were often compelled to work in German factories. Despite the occupation, many French citizens formed a resistance movement to oppose both the German and Vichy governments through acts of sabotage, intelligence gathering, and support for various Allied airmen shot down over France. General Charles de Gaulle, who had fled to London, rallied the Free French Forces and called for resistance against the Axis Powers. These units participated in Allied campaigns in North Africa, Italy, and the final push into Germany.

The turning point for France came on June 6, 1944, with the Allied invasion of Normandy, known colloquially as D-Day. This marked the beginning of the liberation of Western Europe. Paris was freed in August of that same year, and the Allies continued to advance through France. Though the British and Americans are often remembered as the liberators, French forces were integral in freeing many French cities, including Marseille and Lyon. When Germany at last surrendered in May 1945, France was counted among the victorious Allied nations and happily cast off the shackles of German occupation.

Despite the existence of an active resistance movement during World War II, the presence of collaborators with Nazi Germany within France could not be ignored. After the war, France faced a reckoning known as the *Épuration légale* (Legal Purge), where conspirators were prosecuted. The Vichy regime's role remained a controversial and sensitive topic in post-war France, and it would take time to come to terms with the part Vichy France played in Nazi goals and the Holocaust as a whole.

With the war ending, France, Europe, and much of the world had rebuilding to do. The Marshall Plan, which provided economic assistance to Europe from the United States, helped to give France the funds needed to gradually recover. In an attempt to hopefully stop the next Hitler, the United Nations (UN) was formed as the successor organization to the League of Nations. France became a founding member.

Though the Third Republic had been decidedly ended by the Nazi invasion and occupation, France carried onward with the Fourth Republic beginning in 1946. As the nation moved into the second half of the twentieth century, many colonies they had fought to secure during the nineteenth and early twentieth centuries were no longer willing to allow a foreign nation to rule over them. A decolonization process began in Africa and was hastened by the Algerian War of Independence from 1954 to 1962. The fighting here was brutal and bloody, and after the horrors of the last two world wars, France did not have the stomach to continue onward. In 1959, Charles de Gaulle, now the newly elected President of France, conceded that the Algerians had every right to rule their own land. An agreement between Algeria and France was reached in 1962, and the country won independence.

Before the Algerian War of Independence, France had also left Asia. French Indochina, a federation of what is now Vietnam, Cambodia, and Laos, had been under France's control since the nineteenth century. However, beginning almost immediately after the conclusion of World War II, France attempted to reassert control over its Asian colonies, resulting in the First Indochina War (1946–1954). Facing resistance from nationalist movements, particularly the Viet Minh led by (Ho Chi Minh) in Vietnam, the French were defeated at the Battle of Dien Bien Phu in 1954. France agreed to leave the region, establishing the Geneva Accords, which partitioned Vietnam along the 17th parallel. The North was to stay under communist control, while the South remained non-communist. Though this event marked the end of French colonial rule in Asia, it also set the stage for subsequent conflicts, notably the Vietnam War.

Another factor that led to France releasing Indochina, Algeria, and their other colonies was the political instability at home. The Fourth Republic was plagued by economic challenges and was ineffective, evidenced by frequent leadership changes. In 1958, while France was in the midst of dealing with Algeria, things became so unstable back at home that there was the possibility of military intervention. Charles de Gaulle, the hero of World War II, was called back into power to address the crisis. De Gaulle proposed a new constitution that concentrated executive power in the presidency, formed a stronger executive branch, aimed to address the perceived weaknesses of the parliamentary system, and provided a more decisive and stable government for France. This change was approved by a referendum, and the Fifth Republic was inaugurated on October 4, 1958, with Charles de Gaulle behind the wheel as the new president.

For better or worse, De Gaulle was a stabilizing force in French politics. The Fifth Republic that he established at the end of the 1950s is still the reigning republic in 2020s France, and the nation has enjoyed a relatively smooth transfer of power between presidents. Furthermore, while de

Gaulle was in office, France enjoyed a period of economic growth known as the *Trente Glorieuses* (the Glorious Thirty) —a thirty-year-long spell of modernization and prosperity.

Culturally, the 1960s brought about the Nouvelle Vague (New Wave) in cinema, with filmmakers like Jean-Luc Godard and François Truffaut challenging traditional cinematic conventions. They often used unusual storytelling techniques, improvised dialogue, and handheld cameras to create a more natural and spontaneous feel in their films. The movement profoundly impacted the global cinematic landscape, influencing subsequent generations of filmmakers and contributing to the evolution of modern filmmaking styles. Socially, there were significant student and worker protests in May 1968 advocating for more democratic and participatory structures. While the protests did not result in a revolution, they did have a lasting impact on French society, prompting social reforms and contributing to a more liberal cultural atmosphere.

On the international front, France was a founding member of the European Economic Community (EEC), which was a significant step toward European integration and cooperation. Formed by the Treaty of Rome on March 25, 1957, the original members of the EEC were France, West Germany, Italy, Belgium, the Netherlands, and Luxembourg. Mostly, the EEC existed to create a common market and eliminate trade barriers among its member states. This fostered economic integration by allowing the free movement of goods, services, capital, and labor across national borders. Furthermore, it was hoped that greater connectivity among member nations would prevent the recurrence of devastating conflicts that had plagued Europe in the first half of the 20th century.

Around the same time, two other organizations, the European Atomic Energy Community (EURATOM) and the European Coal and Steel Community (ECSC), were formed. Over time, these communities, coupled with the EEC, evolved into the European Union (EU) with the Maastricht Treaty in 1992.

Despite France's role as a founding member of the EEC, the nation did not always stay in lockstep with various allies. Developing its own nuclear weapons and pursuing an independent defense policy, France withdrew from the North Atlantic Treaty Organization (NATO)'s integrated military command in 1966 after disagreements with the United States, though it did rejoin in 2009.

When the *Trente Glorieuses* petered out by the mid-1970s, France faced familiar economic challenges, including periods of recession and attempts at economic reforms. The end of the post-war economic boom and the ensuing contraction sparked labor strikes and social unrest. Prior to the 1970s, the Fifth Republic had largely been ruled by moderate to right-wing conservative factions. The changing climate of the decade led to the rise of left-wing movements, exemplified by the election of Valéry Giscard d'Estaing and his successor, François Mitterrand. D'Estaing emphasized modernization and economic liberalization. His regime also saw a relaxed stance on multiple social issues like abortion, contraception, and divorce.

The drift leftward continued under Mitterrand, a member of the Socialist Party and the first left-wing president of the

Fifth Republic. He implemented a series of socialist reforms, namely increasing social benefits, abolishing the death penalty, and lifting the minimum wage. Several financial and industrial institutions were also nationalized under Mitterrand. Unfortunately, Mitterrand's policies caused economic woes for France— particularly inflation. By 1983, the Mitterrand government was forced to shift toward more centrist policies known as the *tournant de la rigueur* (austerity turn). The Socialist Party, in response to the economic climate of the 1980s, became far less socialist in actuality, espousing free-market liberalism and turning away from core socialist principles.

Due to high unemployment and public debt, and also likely due in part to the Socialist Party losing its identity, the political pendulum in France swung rightward during the 1990s under the presidency of Jacques Chirac. Though moderates still reigned supreme, there was a marked increase in interest in far-right ideology, as evidenced by the surprising success of far-right candidate Jean-Marie Le Pen in 2002. Liberalizing the economy, reducing the role of the state, and encouraging privatization were all on the menu. However, the French people pushed back against pension and welfare reforms, with public sector workers going on strike in December 1995. There were also concerns about workers' welfare and rights amid an increasingly globalizing world influenced by multinational corporations. The rapid advance of technology during the 1990s and early 2000s also shaped new business practices, changes in communication, and innovations in entertainment.

France remained a prominent voice in Europe and on the world stage, signing the Maastricht Treaty in 1992 to establish the European Union (EU). Ten years later, France abandoned their national currency in favor of the euro—the official currency of the EU—showcasing the nation's continued willingness to participate in the broader context of Europe rather than attend solely to its own national interests. France also actively participates in the United Nations (UN), sending people worldwide to join various peacekeeping missions.

Recently, France has vacillated between alternating periods of conservative and socialist presidencies, though Emmanuel Macron, elected in 2017, represents a centrist political approach. However, the political climate and public opinion in France have been affected and defined by several high-profile terrorist attacks, mostly in 2015 and 2016. The most notable was the Île-de-France attack from January 7 to 9, 2015, which included the *Charlie Hebdo* shooting; the November 2015 shootings and suicide bombings at the Bataclan and Stade de France along with other venues in Paris; and the July 2016 vehicle ramming at a Bastille Day celebration in Nice. These events have, understandably, raised concerns about national security and led to debates on how best to handle counterterrorism measures.

The citizens have also maintained their reputation as people willing to strike, riot, and disrupt society when necessary. The 2018 Yellow Vest Protests are a prime example of this, with French citizens taking to the streets to protest financial inequalities and to demand social and economic reforms. The movement highlighted a general air of social discontent that has yet to be addressed. This did not slow down in the 2020s, despite the intervention of the COVID-19 pandemic, which caused widespread lockdowns and concerns, though the swift development of a vaccine helped address the severity of the disease. 2023 saw the worst period of rioting in almost two decades. Worries over financial inequality, climate change, living conditions, and a bedbug infestation during the summer fueled discontent and unrest.

Yet, despite all these challenges, France has remained a cultural giant on the world's stage. New movements in cinema, literature, philosophy, fashion, and more often find a welcoming home in France. After the *Nouvelle Vague* in cinema in the 1960s, the 1980s saw the rise of *Cinéma du Look*—a movement characterized by visually stylish and emotionally charged films. Directors such as Jean-Jacques Beineix and Luc Besson played pivotal roles. In recent years, French cinema has continued to produce internationally acclaimed films, with directors like Olivier Assayas and Abdellatif Kechiche receiving recognition.

In literature, new voices have thrived from the 1980s onward. Novelists like Milan Kundera (*The Unbearable Lightness of Being*) and Marguerite Duras (*The Lover*) explored the human experience from a new perspective. Philosophers like Jacques Derrida and his philosophy of deconstruction were highly influential to the intellectual discourse of the late twentieth and early twenty-first centuries.

France has continuously maintained its reputation as a global fashion capital. Paris Fashion Week, a tradition since the 1970s, remains a premier event showcasing the creations of renowned designers. The twentieth century saw the rise of many of fashion's biggest names and houses: Coco Chanel,

Christian Dior, Jean Paul Gaultier, Yves Saint Laurent, and Hubert de Givenchy. Though a historically significant fashion capital, Paris remains supportive of contemporary designers who continue to push boundaries in fashion.

Musically, France really came alive in the 1980s with the rise of French pop and electronic music. Artists like Jean-Michel Jarre and Mylène Farmer achieved international success, and others like the electronic dance music duo Daft Punk have followed in their footsteps. In recent years, hip-hop has become the dominant force in French music, gaining popularity within the nation as well as globally. Additionally, as new populations immigrate to France, the music scene has become increasingly diverse, incorporating influences from Africa, the Caribbean, and other regions with significant French connections.

Contemporary visual art in France has been characterized by a diverse range of styles and movements. The Centre Pompidou[23] in Paris opened in the late 1970s and became a hub for modern and contemporary art. Creators like Sophie Calle and the street artist and photographer JR[25] have exemplified modern innovation in the field of visual art.

In a nation with as long an artistic history as France, the country has done a fantastic job of combining preservation with modern innovation. An excellent example is the Louvre; originally a medieval fortress constructed by King Philip II, it has morphed over the years into a stunning art museum home to wonders like the *Mona Lisa* and the *Nike of Samothrace*. The most recent architectural addition to the Louvre is the iconic Louvre Pyramid[26], designed by Chinese-American architect I. M. Pei, and it has become a powerful symbol of architectural prowess. However, as climate concerns grow increasingly important to the French populace, the architectural trends of the twenty-first century have seen the rise of sustainable and eco-friendly building design.

Though famously interested in safeguarding its traditional language, cultures, and customs, France has been greatly enriched by recognizing and promoting cultural diversity. Many people from former French colonies like Senegal and Tunisia have immigrated to Europe, finding a home in France and bringing their own vibrant cultural traditions with them.

As with the rest of the world, change is on the horizon. The challenges of climate change, migration, and the global economy's interconnectedness make one country a problem for all. France is a nation of resilient people willing to stand up for what they need. If history is any indication, France and its people will rise to meet the challenges of the twenty-first century in their unique way, with style, intensity, and directness.

As we close this rich tapestry of France's history, we are reminded that history is not just about the past; it's a continuous thread that weaves into the present and shapes the future. France, with its remarkable resilience and distinctive flair, stands at the crossroads of a rapidly evolving world, ready to confront the challenges and seize the opportunities that lie ahead.

Your journey through the pages of this book is a testament to your interest in understanding the forces that have shaped nations and the world. If you found this exploration enlightening, thought-provoking, or even if you have suggestions for improvement, I would be deeply appreciative if you could take a moment to share your thoughts in a review. Your feedback is not just valuable; it's the beacon that guides authors and historians in their quest to illuminate the past and offer perspectives for the future.

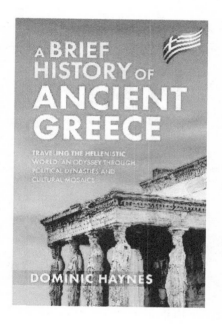

A Brief History of Ancient Greece: Traveling the Hellenistic World:
An Odyssey Through Political Dynasties and Cultural Mosaics

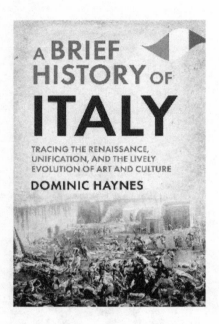

A Brief History of Italy: Tracing the Renaissance, Unification, and the Lively Evolution of Art and Culture

A BRIEF HISTORY OF CENTRAL BANKING

HOW THE QUEST FOR FINANCIAL
STABILITY LED TO UNCONVENTIONAL
MONETARY PRACTICES

DOMINIC HAYNES

A Brief History of Central Banking: How the Quest for Financial
Stability Led to Unconventional Monetary Practices

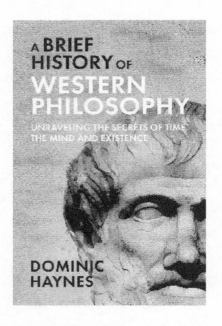

A Brief History of Western Philosophy: Unraveling the Secrets of
Time, the Mind, and Existence

REFERENCES

Adams, S. (2023, September 12). *Battle of Poitiers. Encyclopedia Britannica.* https://www.britannica.com/event/Battle-of-Poitiers-French-history-1356

Bouloiseau, M. (2023, October 9). *Maximilien Robespierre. Encyclopedia Britannica.* https://www.britannica.com/biography/Maximilien-Robespierre

Britannica, T. Editors of Encyclopaedia (2023, November 24). *Albigenses. Encyclopedia Britannica.* https://www.britannica.com/topic/Albigenses

Britannica, T. Editors of Encyclopaedia (2023, May 15). *Alcuin. Encyclopedia Britannica.* https://www.britannica.com/biography/Alcuin

Britannica, T. Editors of Encyclopaedia (2023, December 18). *Algerian War. Encyclopedia Britannica.* https://www.britannica.com/event/Algerian-War

Britannica, T. Editors of Encyclopaedia (2023, October 17). *Anjou. Encyclopedia Britannica.* https://www.britannica.com/place/Anjou

Britannica, T. Editors of Encyclopaedia (2023, December 20). *Anne of Austria. Encyclopedia Britannica.* https://www.britannica.com/biography/Anne-of-Austria

Britannica, T. Editors of Encyclopaedia (2017, August 23). *Aquitaine. Encyclopedia Britannica.* https://www.britannica.com/place/Aquitaine

Britannica, T. Editors of Encyclopaedia (2023, November 9). *Arianism. Encyclopedia Britannica.* https://www.britannica.com/topic/Arianism

Britannica, T. Editors of Encyclopaedia (2023, January 1). *Arius. Encyclopedia Britannica.* https://www.britannica.com/biography/Arius

Britannica, T. Editors of Encyclopaedia (2016, November 11). *Arverni. Encyclopedia Britannica.* https://www.britannica.com/topic/Arverni

Britannica, T. Editors of Encyclopaedia (2011, September 28). *Austrasia. Encyclopedia Britannica.* https://www.britannica.com/place/Austrasia

Britannica, T. Editors of Encyclopaedia (2017, December 26). *Auvergne. Encyclopedia Britannica.* https://www.britannica.com/place/Auvergne

Britannica, T. Editors of Encyclopaedia (2023, January 1). *Baldwin I. Encyclopedia Britannica.* https://www.britannica.com/biography/Baldwin-I-count-of-Flanders

Britannica, T. Editors of Encyclopaedia (2023, November 17). *Battle of Waterloo*. *Encyclopedia Britannica*. https://www.britannica.com/event/Battle-of-Waterloo

Britannica, T. Editors of Encyclopaedia (2007, July 6). *Belgica*. *Encyclopedia Britannica*. https://www.britannica.com/place/Belgica-ancient-province-Europe

Britannica, T. Editors of Encyclopaedia (2023, November 24). *Burgundy*. *Encyclopedia Britannica*. https://www.britannica.com/place/Burgundy

Britannica, T. Editors of Encyclopaedia (2023, November 30). *Carloman*. *Encyclopedia Britannica*. https://www.britannica.com/biography/Carloman-king-of-the-Franks-751-771

Britannica, T. Editors of Encyclopaedia (2023, January 1). *Charles I*. *Encyclopedia Britannica*. https://www.britannica.com/biography/Charles-I-duke-of-Lower-Lorraine

Britannica, T. Editors of Encyclopaedia (2023, October 2). *Charles II*. *Encyclopedia Britannica*. https://www.britannica.com/biography/Charles-II-Holy-Roman-emperor

Britannica, T. Editors of Encyclopaedia (2023, December 12). *Charles VIII*. *Encyclopedia Britannica*. https://www.britannica.com/biography/Charles-VIII

Britannica, T. Editors of Encyclopaedia (2023, December 24). *Charles Of France*. *Encyclopedia Britannica*. https://www.britannica.com/biography/Charles-of-France

Britannica, T. Editors of Encyclopaedia (2023, November 12). *Charles Maurras*. *Encyclopedia Britannica*. https://www.britannica.com/biography/Charles-Maurras

Britannica, T. Editors of Encyclopaedia (2023, October 12). *Cisalpine Gaul*. *Encyclopedia Britannica*. https://www.britannica.com/place/Cisalpine-Gaul

Britannica, T. Editors of Encyclopaedia (2023, August 28). *Clément Marot*. *Encyclopedia Britannica*. https://www.britannica.com/biography/Clement-Marot

Britannica, T. Editors of Encyclopaedia (2023, February 22). *Commune*. *Encyclopedia Britannica*. https://www.britannica.com/topic/commune-medieval-Western-Europe

Britannica, T. Editors of Encyclopaedia (2024, January 5). *Commune of Paris*. *Encyclopedia Britannica*. https://www.britannica.com/event/Commune-of-Paris-1871

Britannica, T. Editors of Encyclopaedia (2023, April 13). *Council of*

Chalcedon. *Encyclopedia Britannica*. https://www.britannica.com/event/Council-of-Chalcedon

Britannica, T. Editors of Encyclopaedia (2019, July 25). *Councils of Ephesus. Encyclopedia Britannica*. https://www.britannica.com/event/councils-of-Ephesus

Britannica, T. Editors of Encyclopaedia (2023, September 19). *Fatimid dynasty. Encyclopedia Britannica*. https://www.britannica.com/topic/Fatimid-dynasty

Britannica, T. Editors of Encyclopaedia (2019, July 30). *First Council of Constantinople. Encyclopedia Britannica*. https://www.britannica.com/event/First-Council-of-Constantinople-381

Britannica, T. Editors of Encyclopaedia (2023, April 26). *Francesco Primaticcio. Encyclopedia Britannica*. https://www.britannica.com/biography/Francesco-Primaticcio

Britannica, T. Editors of Encyclopaedia (2023, January 1). *François Clouet. Encyclopedia Britannica*. https://www.britannica.com/biography/Francois-Clouet

Britannica, T. Editors of Encyclopaedia (2024, January 4). *François Mitterrand. Encyclopedia Britannica*. https://www.britannica.com/biography/Francois-Mitterrand

Britannica, T. Editors of Encyclopaedia (2023, August 31). *Frank. Encyclopedia Britannica*. https://www.britannica.com/topic/Frank-people

Britannica, T. Editors of Encyclopaedia (2014, February 5). *The Fronde. Encyclopedia Britannica*. https://www.britannica.com/event/The-Fronde

Britannica, T. Editors of Encyclopaedia (2023, November 10). *Gallia Comata. Encyclopedia Britannica*. https://www.britannica.com/place/Gallia-Comata

Britannica, T. Editors of Encyclopaedia (2023, July 28). *Gallic Wars. Encyclopedia Britannica*. https://www.britannica.com/event/Gallic-Wars

Britannica, T. Editors of Encyclopaedia (2023, August 20). *Gaspard II de Coligny, seigneur de Châtillon. Encyclopedia Britannica*. https://www.britannica.com/biography/Gaspard-II-de-Coligny-seigneur-de-Chatillon

Britannica, T. Editors of Encyclopaedia (2023, November 10). *Gaul. Encyclopedia Britannica*. https://www.britannica.com/place/Gaul-ancient-region-Europe

Britannica, T. Editors of Encyclopaedia (2023, July 14). *Geneva Accords. Encyclopedia Britannica*. https://www.britannica.com/event/Geneva-Accords

Britannica, T. Editors of Encyclopaedia (2018, April 2). *Helvetii*. *Encyclopedia Britannica*. https://www.britannica.com/topic/Helvetii

Britannica, T. Editors of Encyclopaedia (2023, November 19). *Henry IV*. *Encyclopedia Britannica*. https://www.britannica.com/biography/Henry-IV-king-of-England

Britannica, T. Editors of Encyclopaedia (2015, July 9). *Holy League*. *Encyclopedia Britannica*. https://www.britannica.com/topic/Holy-League-French-history

Britannica, T. Editors of Encyclopaedia (2023, December 1). *Hugh Capet*. *Encyclopedia Britannica*. https://www.britannica.com/biography/Hugh-Capet

Britannica, T. Editors of Encyclopaedia (2023, October 13). *Hundred Years' War*. *Encyclopedia Britannica*. https://www.britannica.com/event/Hundred-Years-War

Britannica, T. Editors of Encyclopaedia (2023, September 26). *Italian Wars*. *Encyclopedia Britannica*. https://www.britannica.com/event/Italian-Wars

Britannica, T. Editors of Encyclopaedia (2023, May 14). *Jacquerie*. *Encyclopedia Britannica*. https://www.britannica.com/event/Jacquerie

Britannica, T. Editors of Encyclopaedia (2023, February 25). *Jacques Lefèvre d'Étaples*. *Encyclopedia Britannica*. https://www.britannica.com/biography/Jacques-Lefevre-dEtaples

Britannica, T. Editors of Encyclopaedia (2019, October 31). *Jean Clouet*. *Encyclopedia Britannica*. https://www.britannica.com/biography/Jean-Clouet

Britannica, T. Editors of Encyclopaedia (2023, April 13). *John II*. *Encyclopedia Britannica*. https://www.britannica.com/biography/John-II-king-of-France

Britannica, T. Editors of Encyclopaedia (2023, December 14). *Languedoc*. *Encyclopedia Britannica*. https://www.britannica.com/place/Languedoc

Britannica, T. Editors of Encyclopaedia (2023, October 9). *La Tène*. *Encyclopedia Britannica*. https://www.britannica.com/place/La-Tene

Britannica, T. Editors of Encyclopaedia (2008, October 20). *Ligurian*. *Encyclopedia Britannica*. https://www.britannica.com/topic/Ligurian

Britannica, T. Editors of Encyclopaedia (2023, September 14). *Louis VII*. *Encyclopedia Britannica*. https://www.britannica.com/biography/Louis-VII

Britannica, T. Editors of Encyclopaedia (2023, November 4). *Louis VIII*. *Encyclopedia Britannica*. https://www.britannica.com/biography/Louis-VIII

Britannica, T. Editors of Encyclopaedia (2023, November 20). *Louis XII. Encyclopedia Britannica.* https://www.britannica.com/biography/Louis-XII

Britannica, T. Editors of Encyclopaedia (2023, November 30). *Louis XV. Encyclopedia Britannica.* https://www.britannica.com/biography/Louis-XV

Britannica, T. Editors of Encyclopaedia (2023, October 2). *Louis-Philippe. Encyclopedia Britannica.* https://www.britannica.com/biography/Louis-Philippe

Britannica, T. Editors of Encyclopaedia (2015, January 11). *Lugdunensis. Encyclopedia Britannica.* https://www.britannica.com/place/Lugdunensis

Britannica, T. Editors of Encyclopaedia (2023, January 1). *Marcus Cassianius Latinius Postumus. Encyclopedia Britannica.* https://www.britannica.com/biography/Marcus-Cassianius-Latinius-Postumus

Britannica, T. Editors of Encyclopaedia (2018, May 1). *Narbonensis. Encyclopedia Britannica.* https://www.britannica.com/place/Narbonensis

Britannica, T. Editors of Encyclopaedia (2023, November 28). *Philippe II, duc d'Orléans. Encyclopedia Britannica.* https://www.britannica.com/biography/Philippe-II-duc-dOrleans

Britannica, T. Editors of Encyclopaedia (2022, December 12). *Pippin II. Encyclopedia Britannica.* https://www.britannica.com/biography/Pippin-II-Carolingian-mayor

Britannica, T. Editors of Encyclopaedia (2017, September 22). *Poitou. Encyclopedia Britannica.* https://www.britannica.com/place/Poitou

Britannica, T. Editors of Encyclopaedia (2023, October 11). *Raymond Poincaré. Encyclopedia Britannica.* https://www.britannica.com/biography/Raymond-Poincare

Britannica, T. Editors of Encyclopaedia (2023, July 6). *René I. Encyclopedia Britannica.* https://www.britannica.com/biography/Rene-I

Britannica, T. Editors of Encyclopaedia (2023, December 18). *Revolutions of 1848. Encyclopedia Britannica.* https://www.britannica.com/event/Revolutions-of-1848

Britannica, T. Editors of Encyclopaedia (2023, June 11). *Robert I. Encyclopedia Britannica.* https://www.britannica.com/biography/Robert-I-king-of-France

Britannica, T. Editors of Encyclopaedia (2023, November 10). *Rosso Fiorentino. Encyclopedia Britannica.* https://www.britannica.com/biography/Rosso-Fiorentino

Britannica, T. Editors of Encyclopaedia (2020, April 23). *Saint Zacharias.*

Encyclopedia Britannica. https://www.britannica.com/biography/Saint-Zacharias

Britannica, T. Editors of Encyclopaedia (2017, April 2). *School of Fontainebleau. Encyclopedia Britannica.* https://www.britannica.com/art/school-of-Fontainebleau

Britannica, T. Editors of Encyclopaedia (2019, September 6). *Treaties of Nijmegen. Encyclopedia Britannica.* https://www.britannica.com/event/Treaties-of-Nijmegen

Britannica, T. Editors of Encyclopaedia (2024, January 2). *Treaty of Versailles. Encyclopedia Britannica.* https://www.britannica.com/event/Treaty-of-Versailles-1919

Britannica, T. Editors of Encyclopaedia (2022, November 14). *Triple Alliance. Encyclopedia Britannica.* https://www.britannica.com/event/Triple-Alliance-Europe-1882-1915

Britannica, T. Editors of Encyclopaedia (2016, March 1). *Urnfield culture. Encyclopedia Britannica.* https://www.britannica.com/topic/Urnfield-culture

Britannica, T. Editors of Encyclopaedia (2011, May 20). *Veneti. Encyclopedia Britannica.* https://www.britannica.com/topic/Veneti-Celtic-people

Bubonic Plague: The First Pandemic. (2019, April 25). Science Museum. https://www.sciencemuseum.org.uk/objects-and-stories/medicine/bubonic-plague-first-pandemic

Buttinger, J., Osborne, M., Turley, W., et al. (2024, January 5). *Vietnam. Encyclopedia Britannica.* https://www.britannica.com/place/Vietnam

Cartwright, M. (2021, April 1). *Ancient Celts.* World History Encyclopedia. https://www.worldhistory.org/celt/

Cartwright, M. (2020, August 24). *Chateau de Chambord.* World History Encyclopedia. https://www.worldhistory.org/Chateau_de_Chambord/

Cartwright, M. (2018, October 22). *Council of Clermont.* World History Encyclopedia. https://www.worldhistory.org/Council_of_Clermont/

Cartwright, M. (2018, July 9). *First Crusade.* World History Encyclopedia. https://www.worldhistory.org/First_Crusade/

Cartwright, M. (2021, March 30). *Hallstatt Culture.* World History Encyclopedia. https://www.worldhistory.org/Hallstatt_Culture/

Cartwright, M. (2021, March 31). *La Tène Culture.* World History Encyclopedia. https://www.worldhistory.org/La_Tene_Culture/

Contreni, J. (2023, October 6). *Louis I. Encyclopedia Britannica.* https://www.britannica.com/biography/Louis-I-Holy-Roman-emperor

Cunliffe, B. and Koch, J. (2010). *Celtic from the West: Alternative Perspectives from Archaeology, Genetics, Language and Literature.* Oxbow Books. doi. org/10.2307/j.ctv13pk64k

Dodman, B. (2023, December 28). *Riots, protests and climate uprisings: 2023 was a tumultuous year in France.* France 24. https://www.france24.com/en/france/20231228-riots-protests-and-climate-uprisings-2023-was-a-tumultuous-year-in-france

Drinkwater, J., Bernard, F., Flower, J., et al. (2024, January 5). *France. Encyclopedia Britannica.* https://www.britannica.com/place/France

Duckett, E. (2023, October 18). *Charles Martel. Encyclopedia Britannica.* https://www.britannica.com/biography/Charles-Martel

Duckett, E. (2023, October 25). *Pippin III. Encyclopedia Britannica.* https://www.britannica.com/biography/Pippin-III

Erlanger, P. (2023, December 7). *Louis XIV. Encyclopedia Britannica.* https://www.britannica.com/biography/Louis-XIV-king-of-France

Euler, H. (2024, January 5). *Napoleon III. Encyclopedia Britannica.* https://www.britannica.com/biography/Napoleon-III-emperor-of-France

Fischer, C., Pemonge, M., Ducoussau, I., et al. (2022, April 15). Origin and mobility of Iron Age Gaulish groups in present-day France revealed through archaeogenomics. iScience 25(4). https://doi.org/10.1016/j.isci.2022.104094

Franco, C. (2023, December 1). *Diocletian.* History Cooperative. https://historycooperative.org/gaius-aurelius-valerius-diocletianus/

Gallic Wars. (n.d.). *Gallic Wars.* History Maps. https://history-maps.com/story/Gallic-Wars

Gibbons, A. (2021, December 22). *Early migration from France may have brought Celtic languages to Britain.* Science. https://www.science.org/content/article/early-migration-france-may-have-brought-celtic-languages-britain

Godechot, J. (2024, January 3). *Napoleon I. Encyclopedia Britannica.* https://www.britannica.com/biography/Napoleon-I

Groeneveld, E. (2016, September 6). *Lascaux Cave.* World History Encyclopedia. https://www.worldhistory.org/Lascaux_Cave/

History.com Editors. (2019, October 24). *Who Were Celts.* History.com. https://www.history.com/topics/european-history/celts

History.com Editors. (2023, August 11). *World War I.* History.com.https://www.history.com/topics/world-war-i/world-war-i-history

Hudson, M. (2022, March 8). *Battle of Alesia. Encyclopedia Britannica.* https://www.britannica.com/event/Battle-of-Alesia-52-BCE

Kiger, P. (2023, April 19). *How Many People Died in World War I?.* History.com.https://www.history.com/news/how-many-people-died-in-world-war-i

Kneale, A. (2020, July 4). *Origin of the Celts: "Celtic From The West" Theory Puts Celtic Homelands on Western European Atlantic Coast.* Transceltic. https://www.transceltic.com/pan-celtic/origin-celts

Kulik, R. M. (2023, September 27). *Carolingian Renaissance. Encyclopedia Britannica.* https://www.britannica.com/topic/Carolingian-Renaissance

Levron, J. (2023, September 28). *Louis IX. Encyclopedia Britannica.* https://wwww.britannica.com/biography/Louis-IX

Mark, H. (2023, May 18). *Coup of 18 Brumaire.* World History Encyclopedia. https://www.worldhistory.org/Coup_of_18_Brumaire/

Mark, H. (2023, March 20). *Franks.* World History Encyclopedia. https://www.worldhistory.org/Franks/

Mark, H. (2023, January 27). *French Directory.* World History Encyclopedia. https://www.worldhistory.org/French_Directory/

Mark, H. (2023, April 19). *Napoleon's Italian Campaign.* World History Encyclopedia. https://www.worldhistory.org/Napoleon's_Italian_-Campaign/

Mark, H. (2022, December 8). *Prairial Uprising.* World History Encyclopedia. https://www.worldhistory.org/Prairial_Uprising/

Mark, H. (2022, December 6). *Thermidorian Reaction.* World History Encyclopedia. https://www.worldhistory.org/Thermidorian_Reaction/

Mark, H. (2023, April 18). *War of the First Coalition.* World History Encyclopedia. https://www.worldhistory.org/War_of_the_First_Coalition/

Mark, H. (2022, December 12). *13 Vendemiaire.* World History Encyclopedia. https://www.worldhistory.org/13_Vendemiaire/

Mark, J. (2014, September 10). *Alemanni.* World History Encyclopedia. https://www.worldhistory.org/alemanni/

Mark, J. (2018, May 31). *Ambiorix.* World History Encyclopedia. https://www.worldhistory.org/ambiorix/

Mark, J. (2014, December 17). *Avars.* World History Encyclopedia. https://www.worldhistory.org/Avars/

Mark, J. (2019, April 2). *Cathars.* World History Encyclopedia. https://www.worldhistory.org/Cathars

Mark, J. (2023, June 16). *Saxon Wars.* World History Encyclopedia. https://www.worldhistory.org/Saxon_Wars/

Mitchell, K. (2023, November 23). *Clovis I. Encyclopedia Britannica.* https://www.britannica.com/biography/Clovis-I

Mollat, M. J. (2023, December 14). *Charles. Encyclopedia Britannica.* https://www.britannica.com/biography/Charles-duke-of-Burgundy

Mollat, M. J. (2023, August 26). *Louis XI. Encyclopedia Britannica.* https://www.britannica.com/biography/Louis-XI

Monnerville, G. (2023, November 20). *Georges Clemenceau. Encyclopedia Britannica.* https://www.britannica.com/biography/Georges-Clemenceau

National Geographic Society. (2023, October 19). *Jan 10, 49 BC: Caesar Crosses the Rubicon.* National Geographic. https://education.nationalgeographic.org/resource/caesar-crosses-rubicon/

National Geographic Society. (2023, October 19). *Julius Caesar.* National Geographic. https://education.nationalgeographic.org/resource/julius-caesar/

Onion, A. (2018, September 1). *Was Germany Doomed in World War I by the Schlieffen Plan?.* History. https://www.history.com/news/was-germany-doomed-in-world-war-i-by-the-schlieffen-plan

Paris attacks: What happened on the night. (2015, December 9). BBC News. https://www.bbc.com/news/world-europe-34818994

Paris Peace Conference. (1919, January). https://history.state.gov/historical documents/frus1919Parisv13

Pernoud, R. (2023, November 17). *Eleanor of Aquitaine. Encyclopedia Britannica.* https://www.britannica.com/biography/Eleanor-of-Aquitaine

Pickles, D. M. (2023, December 27). *Charles de Gaulle. Encyclopedia Britannica.* https://www.britannica.com/biography/Charles-de-Gaulle-president-of-France

Plague. (2022, July 7). World Health Organization. https://www.who.int/news-room/fact-sheets/detail/plague

Popkin, J. D. and Goodwin, A. (2023, December 27). *Louis XVI. Encyclopedia Britannica.* https://www.britannica.com/biography/Louis-XVI

Rasmussen, S., Allentoft, M., Nielsen, K., et al. (2015, October 22). Early Divergent Strains of *Yersinia pestis* in Eurasia 5,000 Years Ago. *Cell,* 163(3): 571-582. DOI: https://doi.org/10.1016/j.cell.2015.10.009

Ray, M. (2019, June 13). *Battle of Tours. Encyclopedia Britannica.* https://www.britannica.com/event/Battle-of-Tours-732

Ritter, R. and Tapié, V. (2023, December 9). *Henry IV. Encyclopedia Britannica.* https://www.britannica.com/biography/Henry-IV-king-of-France

Roos, D. (2023, June 20). *8 Facts About the Celts.* History.com. https://www.history.com/news/celts-facts-ancient-europe

Ross, C. (2023, August 27). *Henry V. Encyclopedia Britannica.* https://www.britannica.com/biography/Henry-V-king-of-England

Saenger, P. (1977). Burgundy and the Inalienability of Appanages in the Reign of Louis XI. *French Historical Studies* 10(1):1-26. Duke University Press. https://doi.org/10.2307/286114

Saller, R., Forsythe, G., Grummond, N., Ferguson, J. Salmon, E., Petit, P., Hornblower, S., Badian, E., MacMullen, R., and Vermeule, E. (2023, November 9). *ancient Rome. Encyclopedia Britannica.* https://www.britannica.com/place/ancient-Rome

Seine-Oise-Marne Culture Overview. (n.d.). Oxford Reference. https://www.oxfordreference.com/display/10.1093/oi/authority.20110803100452587

Shipman, P. (2014, November). The Bright Side of the Black Death. *American Scientist* 102(6):410. DOI: https://doi.org/10.1511/2014.111.410

Sims-Williams, P. (2020, April 2). An Alternative to 'Celtic from the East' and 'Celtic from the West.' *Cambridge Archaeological Journal,* 30(3): 511-529. https://doi.org/10.1017/S0959774320000098

Sorkin, A. (2016, January 2). *The Next Great Famine.* The New Yorker. https://www.newyorker.com/magazine/2016/01/11/the-next-great-famine

Sullivan, R. E. (2023, November 17). *Charlemagne. Encyclopedia Britannica.* https://www.britannica.com/biography/Charlemagne

Sutherland, N. (2023, October 19). *Catherine de' Medici. Encyclopedia Britannica.* https://www.britannica.com/biography/Catherine-de-Medici

Tapié, V. (2023, December 24). *Jean-Baptiste Colbert. Encyclopedia Britannica.* https://www.britannica.com/biography/Jean-Baptiste-Colbert

The Angevin Empire. (n.d.). English Heritage. https://www.english-heritage.org.uk/visit/places/dover-castle/history-and-stories/angevin-empire/

Tobin, R. W. and Moore, W. (2023, December 19). *Molière. Encyclopedia Britannica.* https://www.britannica.com/biography/Moliere-French-dramatist

Tout, T. and Highfield, J.R.L. (2023, November 10). *Edward III. Encyclopedia Britannica.* https://www.britannica.com/biography/Edward-III-king-of-England

Toynbee, A. (2023, November 9). *Julius Caesar*. *Encyclopedia Britannica*. https://www.britannica.com/biography/Julius-Caesar-Roman-ruler

Van der Crabben, J. (2010, July 15). *Migration Age*. World History Encyclopedia. https://www.worldhistory.org/Migration_Age/

Van de Kerkhof, M. (2023, August 22). *The Roman Tetrarchy: An Attempt to Stabilize Rome*. History Cooperative. https://historycooperative.org/roman-tetrarchy/

Wasson, D. (2014, November 10). *Clovis I*. World History Encyclopedia. https://www.worldhistory.org/Clovis_I/

Wasson, D. (2016, March 20). *First Triumvirate*. World History Encyclopedia. https://www.worldhistory.org/First_Triumvirate/

Wasson, D. (2017, March 24). *Postumus*. World History Encyclopedia. https://www.worldhistory.org/Postumus/

Wasson, D. (2017, February 28). *Roman Gaul*. World History Encyclopedia. https://www.worldhistory.org/Roman_Gaul/

Wheelis, M. (2002, September). Biological Warfare at the 1346 Siege of Caffa. *Emerging*
Infectious Diseases 8(9):971-975. DOI: https://doi.org/10.3201/eid0809.010536

Wood, I. N. (2020, May 6). *St. Gregory of Tours*. *Encyclopedia Britannica*. https://www.britannica.com/biography/Saint-Gregory-of-Tours

Made in United States
Orlando, FL
24 April 2024